T0381119

Sharing My Faith in God and His Promise of a Miracle Before It Happens

KATHY PUDER

WESTBOW PRESS*
PRESS*
A DIVISION OF THOMAS NELSON
& ZONDERVAN

WestBow Press books may be ordered through booksellers or by contacting:

WestBow Press
A Division of Thomas Nelson & Zondervan
1663 Liberty Drive
Bloomington, IN 47403
www.westbowpress.com
844-714-3454

All Scripture quotations are taken from the Holy Bible,
NEW INTERNATIONAL VERSION®, NIV® Copyright © 1973, 1978,
1984, 2011 by Biblica, Inc.® Used by permission. All rights reserved worldwide

ISBN: 979-8-3850-0516-1 (sc)
ISBN: 979-8-3850-0517-8 (e)

Library of Congress Control Number: 2023915195

Print information available on the last page.

WestBow Press rev. date: 07/17/2024

I want to first, thank God for His unending love, mercy, and grace He freely gives to all of us. It's amazing to me that His love for us is so much, that He sent His Son to die for us, and if we choose to believe this is true, we will be with Him in heaven when that appointed time comes. Words cannot express how grateful I am that He is allowing me to share with you in advance, my testimony, and His promise to heal me of my seizures that I've had since birth. To my family, I want to thank my husband, Cliff, and our three children, Jackie, Codie, and Sydney, as well as my mom, Pattie, for loving and supporting me always, including this time that I am writing this book. My love for you all, and for God, is never ending. Finally, I wish to thank all of you who read this book. It was written for you. I pray that it is an encouragement to you and your loved ones and helps to inspire you to grow closer in your relationship with God.

Contents

Introduction

How does faith begin? From the time we are little, we learn to put our trust in our teachers to help us to learn, our parents to guide us, and if we live in a Christian household, they teach us to put our trust in God. But what if we don't come from a Christian background, or we are a little older when we start to learn about faith and trust in God? That is OK, because everyone's backstory is different. Our perception of what faith looks like starts at different points in each of our lives. My hope for you is that as time goes by, your faith and trust in God will grow along with your relationship with Him.

As we meet different people from different walks of life, we learn faith has many levels to it, and people can put their faith in many things. For those of us who are believers, we know that above everything and everyone else, our faith in God should come first. When our faith is first, it is amazing to see the beauty He graces His children with, and the testimony that He allows them to share with others when they believe His words, and trust His promise that He had given to them. Displaying your faith for others to see, sharing God's love for them, and encouraging them to grow in, or start their walk with God, is what we are called to do. That is the "why" we are here on earth. Learning and sharing with others about God's love, helping them to know more about Him, and sharing that He has a special purpose for everyone is all a part of "the why."

An example of faith is "action," and sometimes that action

requires you to move when He shares with you audibly and clearly the need to prepare a testimony in advance about how He is going to heal you, before He does it. That is what this book is about. I guess that would be sharing faith before the action. **"Now faith is the confidence in what we hope for and assurance about what we do not see" (Hebrews 11:1).** That is the core mission of this book. It is also my story of how my faith in God has grown over time, how He has told me at different points in time the things that would happen to me, which then did, and how He reminded me again in 2016 that He would heal me of my seizures. At first, I wasn't sure about that, but then I remembered something else He told me eight years earlier, that my mind would remain intact.

The first time He told me this was in 2008, and I will tell you more about that pivotal time later. I'm sure as some of you read this, you're probably thinking, *yeah, right! Did God really tell you that? Do you really believe God spoke to you?* Well, yes. He does have ways of speaking to all of us, and a few of my friends have heard Him speaking to them, too. That's why I'm writing this book, to hopefully help you grow your faith in God. If you do, maybe you will experience the voice of God calling out sometime in your life as well. Our Pastor, Dr. Ike Reighard, whom we refer to as Pastor Ike, sometimes says, "There is a premise for every promise." So this book is a premise for the promise that God has given to me, which will come to fruition whenever God wills it to happen. **Isaiah 38:7 says, "This is the Lord's sign to you that the Lord will do what He has promised."** I promise you, this scripture, which is His Word, is true.

This book is also my thank-you letter to God for His everlasting love and a testimony to share with you about how real He is, how He is a miraculously loving, healing, Heavenly Father available to everyone if they are willing to trust and believe in Him. Another cool and unique thing about God is that He is with every one of us at the same time! His omnipresence is something I've pondered and marveled over many times in my life. His ability to be everywhere and see and hear everyone all at the same time is absolutely amazing to me.

I am grateful to God, and honored to have the opportunity to share my testimony with you about Him in this unique way. I never, ever thought this would be a way I would share my faith with others, but I think it's pretty cool, and I am truly thankful God is allowing me the ability to do so. So, here we go.

1

Where Do We Start?

Where do we start? That is the question I want you to think about. How do you grow in faith if you haven't experienced knowing what faith is? The cool thing is, God created us to naturally embrace faith, which is what we do. Even if you didn't grow up in a house that made church a weekly or multi weekly event, you still have faith in many things, such as knowing the sun will come up in the morning, and the moon will come out at night. Those are events we can expect to happen because we see them happening every day and night. That kind of faith is in seeing, but I'm talking about faith that is unseen. It is experienced by learning about God, the Creator of you and me, and oddly enough, the Creator of everything and everyone too. When we learn who our Creator is, when we know that He created the earth and everything in it, we begin to wonder and want to learn more about Him.

I have always wondered why—why wouldn't people want to learn about Him? It's so easy, and most of us have the access and the capability to do so. Yet, sadly, we don't always take the time or the steps to learn more about Him, such as setting aside some time every day to read His Word through a devotional, a Bible study, or the Bible directly and developing a prayer time along with it. Together, these are unseen, precious moments with God that bring about a relationship with Him when no one else is watching. That is your quiet time, and that is where you grow in your knowledge of who God is. He sees us from afar. He sees us all, and He waits for us to come to Him. He sees the work we do, the good and the bad, the missed opportunities to spend time with Him, as well as the times we reach out to connect with Him. He knows it all. Now, I don't want you to feel uncomfortable, because I, too, had a time when I didn't know about Him. Everyone does, right? For me, it was when I was a kid. Sometimes I would read the colorfully illustrated children's Bible in the doctor's waiting room, but I still didn't know Him as my Heavenly Father—not yet. That didn't happen till I was sixteen. My mom and I moved to Georgia from Texas in 1985. We arrived in the summertime, which gave us time to get acclimated to our new home, the Atlanta traffic, and the roads in Tucker, Georgia, before school started. God is good at preparing you ahead of time for things, which is what He did for me before we moved to Georgia. I just didn't know it at the time, but I will get to that part of the story later.

Anyhoo, the first day in a new school can leave many of us feeling a little anxious and nervous, but for me, I was excited about being in a new state, being close to family again, and having new beginnings in a new school. I was experiencing a lot of new beginnings, which made me feel happy walking into school, instead of anxious. By the way, that is how God wants our relationship with Him to be too. The first day of school was much like what you likely experienced. You walk into the school and watch everyone bustling around and trying to get to their classrooms. People are walking in late and trying to figure out where they're supposed to be. I have to admit, not knowing anyone made me a little anxious, but that changed when a teenage boy named John talked with me during one of my classes, and then invited me to join him and his friends at lunch. We talked about the new school year, the teachers, and our classes. I told them I was new to Georgia. That was exciting to them because they had all grown up in Georgia. I asked them how they became friends. John said they went to church together. I told them that I thought that was cool!

They also told me that they volunteered on Wednesday nights with the Awana program at their church.

I asked them, "What is that?"

John explained, "It is a program that helps kids to learn about God while they get to play and earn points for themselves and their team."

The part that piqued my interest was the fact that it was a program for kids. I loved working with kids, and this sounded like fun. John asked me if I wanted to join them, and I happily said yes!

It was the first of many Wednesday nights that I would spend at church. Seeing the anticipation on the kid's faces and watching them come into the church with their Awana books, ready for us to listen to them memorize their scripture verses, was fun. Then, if they had time, they would do another page in their book and earn more points for themselves and their team. I noticed that each kid was at a different point in their book, and each kid might have a different book depending on how much time they invested in doing their workbooks. I took note of this, observing that the progress in their books showed how much time they spent outside the club learning about God. I also loved the fun crafts they got to make, which always tied in with their lesson. Of course, game time was fun, too, and the volunteers, who were usually us teenagers, quite often were a part of game time. If we weren't physically playing, then we were literally cheering them on! Game time would sometimes get competitive, even for the teenagers, and it was usually when the kids earned most of their points for their team. It was in the midst of all this activity, while I was helping them, that I was learning about God's love for me. I helped them to memorize such scriptures as **Jeremiah 31:3, "I have loved you with an everlasting love"**; **John 15:12, "This is my command, love one another as I have loved you"**; and **Proverbs 3:5–6, "Trust in the Lord with all your heart and lean not on your own understanding, in all your ways acknowledge Him, and He will make your paths straight."** All those scriptures sounded inviting, but then teaching them about why Jesus died for us, helped me to learn more about Him, too.

For God so loved the world that He gave His one and only Son. That whoever believes in Him shall not perish but have everlasting life." (John 3:16)

I am the way and the truth and the life. No one comes to the Father except through me. (John 14:6)

Because the group of kids I was working with were going through their books at about the same pace, I was able to hear the scriptures again and again as we all learned more about Him.

Soon, I had purchased my own Bible and started reading the stories in their entirety. I would look back at the chapters where specific scriptures came from, reading the whole chapter to get the full extent of the content, not just one scripture at a time. Soon, I realized that the more I read, the more I wanted to read, and the more I was learning about what it means to follow Christ. That made me want to ask Jesus for the forgiveness of my sins and ask Him into my heart, which is what I did. Asking Jesus into your heart is a personal decision that you make between you and Him.

The church that I went to at the time had baptisms on Easter. A group lined up along the altar on that Easter Sunday in April 1986, and I was part of it. I had already asked Jesus into my heart, but doing so in public, and being able to do it on Easter, seemed amazing and unique to me. Even before that time in my life I had believed that everything happens for a reason, but from that point on, I would learn that God has a reason for everything—a time and a plan for everything under the sun **(Ecclesiastes 3:1),** even during difficult times. It is in those moments that we can cultivate our relationship with God, and lean more into Him. It is in those difficult moments that He might speak to us if we just believe. Even if we don't, we still might hear His voice. Sometimes in the Bible, He spoke to people who didn't believe in Him so that they would believe. In fact, this morning I read again about Pilate's wife and her dream about Jesus. She pleaded with Pilate to let Jesus go and let Barabbas be the one who died, because by law one of them could be pardoned. In the end, it was Barabbas who was released, and she, who maybe even a day before didn't believe that Jesus was the Messiah, ended up believing that He was. If you happen to read the story, you will notice that Pilate eventually did believe, as his wife did, that Jesus was the Messiah **(Matthew 27:1–66)**. See? Everyday people, as well as leaders of countries, come to believe that Jesus is Lord. When people do, the way they look at the world, and God with His omnipotent power and love for us, changes. The pictures of what we perceive as truth become larger than life. It begins from what we were taught as daily truths, things our parents teach us, then transforms to biblical truths that we learn as we grow in our walk with Him. For each one of us, we can simply exist or desire to know and grow closer to God, and search for the special reason why he created us, the plan and purpose He has waiting for us to discover. It is our decision, though, if we trust Him enough to learn about Him and desire to know what His plan for us is.

All the stories in the Bible are amazing to me. Back then, and even now. Especially the miracles. I have always loved reading about the miracles that occurred throughout the Bible. I have always marveled at the work God does with His hands, by His might, through His power, and by His presence, caring enough to be there for everyone. My mind would always play a visual of the stories in my head, as if I was walking around watching them in real time alongside the ancient biblical people. I know that sounds funny, but that was what it was like for me, feeling like I was surrounded by the Israelites, walking with them through the marketplace or along the Dead Sea or Red Sea, or through Jerusalem, while imagining their journeys.

I hope that God's stories become that real for you as well, because His stories are true. He is so gracious and loving to share them with us so that we can develop a loving, eternal relationship with Him. I truly feel blessed to have been able to learn about Him from a young age and to help kids learn about him too. However, there was another area of my life where I needed His help.

2

Asking for His Help

I GUESS WE DON'T HAVE JUST ONE AREA OF OUR LIVES THAT WE need help with, do we? No, I think not! What I've learned is we each have several areas in our lives where we need guidance and wisdom that go beyond our own understanding.

At the time, my mom was a single parent raising my brother and I. Because she worked long hours, we didn't want to bother her a lot with things we felt we could take care of ourselves, but my grades were one area where I knew I needed help. That is when I started to see God working in my life. I was searching for wisdom, like literally trying to figure out life and school. I remember my Sunday school teacher said, "Proverbs is a book about wisdom. If you want to gain wisdom, read it." Well, I know that seems corny, but I was truly seeking answers for my dilemma, so I started reading in the book of Proverbs.

One day, I was in the library pulling a book off the shelf, thinking about where I was, and stopped. I took a moment to pray to God. "God, please help me to gain wisdom. Please show me how to get my grades up." Shortly after that, I had to go to my science class. That day, my teacher was giving us our graded tests from the previous day. When she gave me my test back, she had a concerned look on her face. She asked me to see her after class, and when I looked at the score on my test, I knew what it was about. I was afraid that she was going to

6

give me grief about my science test and my grade in her class, but, to my surprise, she didn't. Instead, she asked me if I'd ever tried using index cards to study with. I replied, "No, I have never heard of that way of studying before."

She smiled and said, "Try it! It works!" She instructed me to put the questions or vocabulary words on the front, and the answers on the back, and then memorize them, three cards at a time, before going on to the next three, and so on. I smiled, and, yes, the light bulb went off in my head. I thought, *Why didn't I think of that?* I thanked my teacher and let her know that I was truly grateful for her taking the time to help me. I thanked her again after the next test came back, and I had gotten a B, not only in her class but in some of my other classes as well. She wasn't the only one I thanked. I thanked God, too, for being there for me and giving me guidance when I needed it. Even though I still didn't have a clear understanding of how God worked, I paused to recognize that He was there answering my prayer and guiding me as I read His Word. What the index cards were to my studying in school, the time I spent reading the Bible was to my spirit. I was beginning to understand that as I was reading and studying God's Word, I was having fun learning the history of God's people while I was also having fun learning about Him. I was learning that these three things were drawing me into a relationship with Him, and that felt like a great big warm hug wrapped around my soul, which truly felt good.

Feeling the presence of the Holy Spirit is another blessing that comes from knowing God. I felt His presence when I asked for His help in the library and when my teacher helped me, but I also felt a sense of peace every time I went to church. Much later, after I was married, I heard my husband say the same thing when he began to experience church again as an adult. Whether it was Wednesday night or Sunday, or any day of the week, I experienced **"peace that surpasses understanding" (Philippians 4:7)** every time I walked through those church doors, and that peace always felt good.

Even though I have shared with you the excitement of all the new beginnings I was undergoing and how I loved all the new experiences that were happening in my life, I was still trying to work through the normal teenage things and the complexities of unanswered questions that arose not only for me, but for others, too. Such as why people and families go through struggles, why some families break up, or why we can't all just get along. The one question I could answer was how God was different than an earthly father. I could answer this one the same way I already have. I could see that even in my youth, He was there for me when my earthly father was not. I know that for many of you who read this, you may have been blessed with a wonderful, loving, supportive father. If that is you, you are truly blessed. For those who weren't, like my husband and I, God has a different plan for you, and it might be to help someone else get through a situation that might be similar to one you've experienced. Our Sunday school teacher and community pastor, Marlon Longacre, quite often says, "You've gone through what you've been through to help others get through what they're going through." I love hearing him say this because he has a unique "Marlon" way of saying it, but also because it's true, and it aligns with what I've believed since childhood—everything happens for a reason and there is purpose for all things you've experienced. It is God preparing you for your purpose that He created you to walk in and to live out.

Now, if that doesn't encourage you to want to dig into God's Word, that's OK. I hope, though, that by the end of this book, this message might encourage you to get started. For now, I will give you an example of how God started to teach me about Him, even before we moved to Georgia. He was already reaching out to me and helping me to learn about Him, His people—the Israelites, and their culture, Jesus's family's culture, while we were still living in El Paso, Texas.

3

He Is There with You Before You Realize You Know Him

It is December 16, 2020, as I write this chapter, and I am reminiscing on my family's move to El Paso, Texas just when I was starting middle school. When my mom, brother, and I moved there we met, and quickly became friends with our new neighbors, who happened to be Jewish.

Oh, wow! As I'm sitting here writing this, I just realized that the two big moves we made during my childhood were both at points when one would naturally change schools. Both times were during transitional points in time! We first moved to El Paso, Texas, before I started middle school, and then moved to Tucker, Georgia, just before I entered high school! Do you see when you pause for a moment to think back on your life and reflect, how God helped you to connect things in your life with Him at the center it? He will also help you to see His will for you along the way. Isn't that cool? OK, let's get back to the story.

When we moved to El Paso, we moved into an apartment complex. Shortly after, we met a cute little boy standing with his mom outside our apartment. We found out that they lived just a few doors down from us. He was about three or four at the time. My mom and I smiled at him and waved. His grin grew into a great big, adorable smile as he waved back. We said, "Hi," to him and his mom said, "Hi," back to us."

A few days after that, I saw him again, but this time, he was with a girl who was just a little younger than me and who I guessed was his sister. I said hi again to him and introduced myself to her. "Hello, I'm Kathy. I met your little brother and mother the other day."

She smiled and said, "Oh, yes, I heard about you. My name is Talia, and this is my little brother, Benjamin. We call him Ben for short." That would be the first of many meet ups with my new neighbors, because Talia invited me over to her house many times. It was there, at her house with her family, that I would learn about their Jewish heritage, their holidays and traditions, their culture, and their Lord, who later became my Lord too.

I always enjoyed going over there and hanging out with her and her family. It seemed like they were always preparing for some special occasion, even during the times of the year when there weren't any big celebrations. They also seemed to make every day a wonderful gathering of fellowship, even when there wasn't any special reason. Have you ever known a family like that? That was one reason I liked visiting Talia. I also enjoyed just spending time together, like friends do.

I admired the Jewish décor laced throughout their apartment. That first year, I learned so much about the way Orthodox Jews live. Besides learning about their holidays, there were two other things about the way they lived that I thought were unique, and very cool; their eating habits, and their shopping habits, which were correlated together. One of my first visits to Talia's apartment included a trip to the kitchen for a snack. I noticed that they had labels on their cabinets that said "Meat," which was on one side of the kitchen, and "Dairy," which was on the other side. Curiously, I asked Talia why they were there. She said, "Because we are Orthodox Jews, we have two sets of dishes." She opened the cabinets to show me. "We have dinnerware for when we eat meat, and we have a different set we use when we eat dairy."

I was surprised and asked, "So you don't eat cheeseburgers?"

She responded, "Nope! We never have dairy food if we are eating meat that night, and we never mix the plates up either." I thought that was very interesting, except the part about not being able to eat cheeseburgers.

The other interesting thing I learned was how they shopped for food. While we were still in the kitchen, Talia also shared that they only ate food that was kosher, and they only bought food that had a kosher label on it. I was stunned because, of course, all this was new to me. I asked, "How do you know if the food is kosher or not?"

She smiled, got a pickle jar out of the cabinet, and showed me the label. She said, "If it has a 'K' on it like this, if it has a 'U' on it, or if it simply says 'kosher' on it." Well, I thought that was so cool that I decided to go hunting not only at home that night but also the next time my mom and I went to the grocery store, which she still laughs about to this day.

The next time we went grocery shopping, my mother asked me to get some peanut butter. As I picked the jar up, I perused the label and found a "K" on it. I yelled across the aisle, "Hey, Mom! This peanut butter is kosher! We can eat it!"

She laughed and yelled back, "That's awesome! But we aren't Jewish!" I shrunk just a little bit with embarrassment as I noticed other people in the store were laughing at our remarks. Still to this day, that is a happy memory of how I started to realize that there was so much more to my friend's Jewish heritage. Christmas was Hanukkah, and they had a menorah with candles instead of a Christmas tree. For Easter, they didn't have Easter eggs or an Easter bunny. Instead, they had a cross that represented a very important part of their family's history, and just a couple of years after meeting Talia and her family, this cross would become a very important and meaningful part of my life too.

4

When You Connect with Him, He Connects Back

Fast forward from Texas to Georgia and consider where my head was at sixteen years old. I would often think back to those neighbors who so graciously and lovingly taught me about their culture, their lifestyle, their heritage, and their Abba Father, who would become my Abba Father three years later. Please take away from this that God will remind you of where or how He places people in your path to prepare you to grow in your faith. You might not always see it right away, but as you grow in your faith, you will begin to recognize where He places important people or things before you to let you know He is there. That is the Holy Spirit working in you. The further you grow in your walk, the more easily you will notice the little things that seem to come together in your day in a beautiful and uniquely different way.

An example of this happened on December 21, 2020. Sydney and I were going to Walmart to pick up the final things on our list for the kids at the shelter. My oldest daughter, Jackie, had said she wanted to help with the cost of the presents, so at the checkout, I split the gifts up into two groups. I was surprised to notice the totals on the two bills were exactly opposite of each other in numbers. The first total was $65.66, and the second total was $66.65. After noticing this, I held up the receipts to show the cashier. He smiled and said,

"You need to play those numbers." So did the ladies in line behind us. Instead, I went home to look up the biblical meaning behind those numbers. According to my research, the number sixty-five "signifies the love you get from family, and love is the biggest treasure in life-which we all know is true. By loving others, you will be able to be of service in society and help the needy. Your humanitarian nature stems from having a loving character." Interesting, right? It also said that sixty-five signifies "Love and Transformations. A time of leaving the old you behind and focusing in on the new you." I wrote this section on January 2, 2021, at the beginning of the year. A time when we all try to focus on new beginnings.

So, what about the number sixty-six? The number sixty-six "signifies love, compassion, generosity, and determination. It also signifies healing." Healing? Hmm. He truly is a part of our daily lives, walking alongside us. If only we paused longer to see His presence, I wonder what new things we would discover about Him. I sometimes share this statement with others in my Bible studies. These pauses are the moments in life where we stop and go *hmm*. Where we literally ask ourselves, "What is it that I am supposed to learn right now, God? What is God doing in my life?" These pauses, and our new discoveries we learn about Him, are something some Christians experience because they have a relationship with God, which helps them to know there is something bigger going on than the situation they are presently in. When I was a new Christian, I recognized little things like that in my daily life and thought it was the Holy Spirit revealing things to me. Later, as I learned more about it through different Bible studies, I learned that is exactly how the Holy Spirit works! Christians recognize this because they have the presence of the Holy Spirit in their lives because they have asked Jesus into their heart, and into their lives. They also recognize it even more when they study God's word daily and at the same time, are growing in their relationship with Him. It is truly a wonderful blessing to be able to do so.

5

Obedience to God Helps Us to See His Omnipotence

As I write this on January 20, 2021, I am struck by two very profound insights about how being obedient helps us to see God's power. The first one I noticed through Facebook. Joseph Prince had written a three-minute devotion on the importance of writing down your vision by positioning yourself to see God's *hazon* vision. Now many of us have written down goals that we need to accomplish, and that is our vision we can see before us as we look at the paper on which we've written (or typed) our list of goals. But God's "hazon vision," as Joseph Prince mentioned, "refers to a prophetic vision from God Himself, that will surely come to pass."[1] The idea of this may seem far-reaching to some but can be just as real as when you receive an affirmation from someone that gives you guidance and an answer to a situation you may be facing. I have heard our pastor, and many others, mention how they have started writing on one topic but are then led to write about something else entirely. This is something I have recognized myself while putting Sunday school lessons together, facilitating Bible studies, and even as I am writing this book. These are some of the ways the Holy Spirit may guide you.

---

[1] Joseph Prince, "The Hazon Vision," 3:00, www.josephprince.org.

In 2008, during the time we had to leave our home, I experienced this in a uniquely different way that let me know God was giving me a word through my writing, which would later give me affirmation that God was moving us in a new direction as we left our house. Besides the fact that God said He would heal me of my seizures and keep my memory intact, He also told me at that time that I would meet five specific people: Henry Winkler, Corbin Bernsen, Kevin Sorbo, Michael J. Fox, and Mel Gibson.

The thing about affirmations is that they make you think because sometimes the affirmation is so out of the ordinary that it seems impossible, but when God affirms something in your life, then you know God is doing something bigger than you can imagine.

Two weeks after we left our house in Conyers, I met Henry Winkler at a book signing. I was excited to meet him for three reasons. Firstly, because he is the Fonz, of course, but the second reason was that six years earlier, I was trying to develop a specialized computer for dyslexics to help them with their specific needs, and noticed through my research that he has dyslexia, and has an assistant who wrote along with him. I had contacted that assistant back then to ask if I could send the idea for this computer to him, and Mr. Winkler's assistant said, "sure!" It would be years later that some of the program ideas I had for the computer would be developed into apps like Bixby, Google Assistance, Alexa, and Siri. Now the idea for the computer had to be from God because I am not, I repeat, I am *not* literate with computers. It was the educational side that made sense to me.

Anyhoo, when I met Henry Winkler, I introduced myself and asked him if he received the letter I'd sent. He smiled and said, "Yes, I did." As we talked, I enjoyed just the few minutes I had to speak with him because he is such a nice person. I still have his picture on our mantle in our living room. As I said goodbye to him, I realized the third reason why I was excited to meet him, God was giving me an affirmation that day about the first of five people He told me I would meet, as well as it being a good decision to leave the house and everything we owned behind. This last part of my encounter with Mr. Winkler was the one that was the most impactful to me because I was seeing a promise God gave me come true shortly after hearing Him tell me that it would happen.

Shortly after I met Henry Winkler and we left our house in Conyers, there was a casting call for a TV show called *Everyday Edisons*, which was similar to the TV show *Shark Tank*. I went to the casting call to see if they would like the idea of my computer for dyslexics, but it was not one of the inventions they chose to invest in. The good news is that there are apps that are available now to help people with dyslexia, which I like seeing.

Still to this day, I continue to wonder what the specific connection with meeting these five people might be if there even is one. Would we possibly work on some projects together? I still don't know the answer to that, but I always keep it in mind.

Cliff, Henry Winkler, and I at a book signing in 2008.

Corbin Bernsen and I at the International
Kingdomwood Film Festival in 2018.

The next meetings with two of the people God had told me I would meet came to fruition about a decade later. This happened when Sydney and I started serving at a fundraiser for Movieguide. On one occasion, we met Corbin Bernsen, who was working on a film with some of my friends. The following year, Kevin Sorbo came to the fundraiser. As I said hello to them on the red carpet, it started to sink in that God was placing me in a specific area for a specific reason. Your sense for receiving affirmations from God increases the more you experience moments like these. As exciting as it was to meet these wonderful people, I was equally excited and curious as to how these meetings connected with the purpose He has for me, and maybe for them too.

Kevin Sorbo and I at Movieguide's Fundraiser Banquet in 2019

Jackie, Christopher Lloyd, Michael J. Fox,
Sydney, and I at Fan X in 2023.

As I was getting ready to send my manuscript draft to the editors, my girls and I found out there was going to be a comic convention in Utah September 21–23, 2023, and Michael J. Fox and Christopher Lloyd were going to be some of the celebrities you could have the opportunity to meet. We decided to go, and I decided to revise this section of my manuscript on September 27, 2023. Before our trip, I asked God what He wished for me to share with them. For Michael J. Fox, I thought about his research for a cure for Parkinson's disease and thought about essential oils. I then looked up some articles that included specific essential oils that are used to help some people with Parkinson's disease. I included those articles in a letter to him. I also added that if he wanted to, I could interview him to help archive his dad's military story because his dad served in the army.

In my letter to Christopher Lloyd, I shared with him that we had just seen the new movie he was in called *Camp Hideout*. I told him that it was nice seeing him in a faith-based movie and shared with him my friend Trudy Simmons's contact info in case he or his producers wished to connect with her to be interviewed on her show *The Christian View*. I gave them both my Christmas book and told them if I were ever able to get the book turned into a cartoon, I think it would be amazing if they would be some of the voices for the characters.

One thing I've seen through the people I have met, even people who are not mentioned in this chapter, is that God is placing me in certain places to perhaps help people connect with one another and, at the same time, help me to learn how to connect with others better, which is something I really need and want to do. This also ties in with the film projects I'm working on and how they are meant to help us to connect with the people who've made contributions to our country in wonderful ways and hopefully help us all to reconnect better with one another in our families, our communities, around our country, and maybe even around the world. I include in my prayers every day for us all to be able to connect better with one another.

These events make me wonder even more about the things

God said before. Do you see where wondering about God, and then moving, is something He really wants us to do? Wonder in the small moments so we can see what He is doing in the bigger moments. Be obedient to Him, and He will set our paths on a journey that isn't always easy but can be fun and fulfilling beyond anything we can ever imagine.

Now let's get back to Joseph Prince's devotion. He was talking about having time with God and putting aside electronics, Facebook, the TV, and so on to be able to hear from Him. How can we hear from God unless we are in His Word? This is a great question, and you get to learn the answer to that question when you take time to read the Bible. For me, I have always loved spending time in God's Word, I love teaching it, and I love sharing encouragements when I can to help others know how much He loves them. Part of learning for me has been to take notes during my pastor's sermons and during Sunday school. This is what Joseph Prince said to do when you hear God speak. The title of his devotion is "The Importance of Writing Down Your Visions." Now filmmakers do this, but before I became a writer and filmmaker, I did this as a Sunday School teacher. Pastors do this, as well. Joseph Prince was referencing **Habakkuk 2:1–2, which states, "I will stand at my watch and set myself on the rampart and watch to see what He will say to me, and what I will answer when I am corrected. Then my Lord answered me and said: Write down the vision and make it plain on tablets, that He may run who reads it."**

Joseph Prince called this the "hazon vision." I shared this with Marlon, and at the end of my message to Marlon, I wrote, "So this is what it's called when you write things down that you know are from God." This is what I have experienced, he has experienced, and other leaders also experience while doing God's work. They write down what it is God is asking them to do. The prophets did it on tablets, John did it when he wrote Revelation, Paul did it when he wrote his letters, and pastors and writers still do it today. Wow! It has a name! How cool is that? The reason Joseph Prince called it this is because hazon in Hebrew means "vision." I have noticed, as do others, that as we grow in Christ and study His Word, God gives us clarity with things from the Bible. Likewise, it helps you to have more understanding and clarity for you, in your life each and every day.

The second pastoral leader whom I heard from today was Tony Evans. He is a pastor I started listening to when I was in my early twenties. This morning, after messaging Marlon, I was initially going to read my devotion in my Bible study, but I paused and felt the urge to listen to one of Tony Evans's sermons instead. I asked Jackie if she wanted to listen to his sermon with me, and she said sure. So, I turned it on and took notes. Here are my notes from his sermon based on **2 Kings 5:1–17**, the story of Naaman, a valiant soldier and commander for the army of the king of Aram. He was a great warrior but had leprosy, which is an infectious disease that is highly contagious. Now Naaman was not a believer in God, not at first, but he became one when Elisha heard from God to send a messenger to tell him, **"To go wash yourself in the Jordan River seven times."**

As Tony Evans put it, Naaman scoffed, laughed, and then said, "You want me to go into the Jordan River, a very dirty river, and wash myself?" Tony Evans went on to say, "What Naaman viewed as a very gross, dirty river is also where God had provided miracles before in the past. The reason Elisha had him go to the Jordan River is because it's where he has seen miracles happen!"[2] Here are the rest of my notes from Tony Evans's sermon for you to consider.

+ God puts us in situations no man can fix so that we can serve Him.
+ Don't let your dignity prevent you from listening to God.
+ Until your obedience is completed, you cannot expect miracles from God.

---

[2] *The Urban Alternative*, written/performed by Tony Evans, tonyevans.org.

- We need to reject our own opinions and the opinions of others if they're not from God.
- Not only can He cure what's been a problem for years, but He can also take you back to when it wasn't a problem at all.
- Why does God put you in an incurable situation? So that you can find out who God is. Tony Evans said, "He wants to show you when He shows up and shows off. He is in a class by himself."
- When God delivers you from something like this, He reverses you to a baby-like status so you will want God with you wherever you go.

Now when I listened to that last part, I was a little nervous, as sometimes you are when you listen to sermons. It is the uncomfortableness of God's Word where He is speaking to your spirit. It is in those times that you need to pause, reflect, take notes, and consider that these words are God's provision to you. The little moments that cause you to pause and think are the areas you need to pay attention to. They are not always comfortable areas, but you need to push past the discomfort to understand that God has something new for you to learn in your life, something to add to things you already know.

The part of the sermon that made me nervous was, "when I reverse this, you will be like a babe." Now, I know God told me, "I will heal you of your seizures, and your memory will remain intact." I rest on that last part of it, that my memory will remain intact. I hope on it, I believe in it, and I know He will do it because He has done so many things for me that He said He would do and which I am ever so grateful for, but it is the "you will be like a babe." Even as I write this, the direction of my thoughts is changing, and His peace is setting in, going from being afraid that I might sound like a child as a write down my thoughts to understanding that this phrase possibly means looking at the world and the people in the world more from God's point of view. Because I'm already a Christian, I can, instead, have a new perspective. We all can. God encourages us to renew our minds daily **(Romans 12:2; Colossians 3:10)**. It's also one of my daily prayers. It's something I'm continuously asking God to help me with. I can also see where this new perspective might help me in my relationships with others. This is an area in which I continuously pray for myself, my family, and for other families too.

The whole point of sharing this long chapter with you is to show you how when you start praying to Him and seeking Him every day, He will guide you toward the direction He has planned for you, and likewise, your direction toward Him. He has an unconditional love for you that surpasses anything you can ever imagine. He also has a plan for you here on earth to live out that you might miss if you haven't yet trusted in Him or asked Him into your heart, and I don't want you to miss that eternal boat!

6

Obedience to God is Pivotal to God's Plan for You

As I write this chapter in March 2021, I want to remind you of a pivotal time in my life that I briefly mentioned in the introduction but said I would discuss in detail later. Well, here is where you will read about it. The pivotal time I am referring to happened when we were still living in our home in Conyers and we discovered, without a doubt, that we had black mold taking over our house. We had to decide whether we could trust that it all could be removed and restored, or if we would have to leave and lose the house. I knew from my breathing issues and ill health I was experiencing at that time what the right decision was. My husband, on the other hand, was not so sure what we should do. The insurance company argued about the extent of their obligation in the restoration of the house. They argued that we were just imagining it, or maybe we were lying to them about the condition of the house. With all this uncertainty, it made me stop and think. If our house was compromised, and my health, and maybe my family's health was compromised too, then we may have to take all that we own and move it to a new house. But what about all our belongings? They had been exposed to the mold all this time. Wouldn't that just reinfect our new home? I shared my concerns with Cliff, but he said, "We will be OK."

It was shortly after that I became so overwhelmed with my own thoughts of what we were going to do. Which way should we go? Should we take our belongings with us? If so, will we be reinfecting our new environment? What about our health? It was in the middle of all these questions that I heard a loud voice interrupt my thoughts in an instant! The voice was so loud that you would've thought it was a loudspeaker on steroids! Louder than a loudspeaker in a stadium. The deep, deep voice quite simply but very authoritatively said, "Leave everything, and go!" I tremble even as I write this because that voice was ever so present then, just as it is now. Considering I was the only one in the room at the time, I knew in my heart without a doubt whose voice that was. God was telling me very clearly how we should move forward.

We don't always get that loud of a vocal affirmation from God, but when and if you do, you better follow it! Now all I had to do was convince my husband to follow it too. When I first shared with him that I'd heard God and told him what God's voice sounded like, he was still skeptical of course, and said, "Do you really expect us to leave everything we have?" It was then as I heard him speak those words that I realized we were experiencing scripture. **"Leave everything and go" (Luke 14:33).** I knew we needed to be obedient to God. We literally needed to just take our kids and walk away from everything we owned, and that is exactly what I told Cliff we should do! He still was not thrilled with the idea. He still had questions and was confused about what we should do. We decided to have our own testing people come in to test the house to see how bad the mold damage really was.

When the test results came back, the mold levels were so high that our tester confirmed that it would be a good idea, indeed, to leave everything and go. Now, the Bible tells us that other people had to do the same thing sometimes. We all have some area in our lives where we need to let go of things. Sometimes it may be people, habits, things, or even professions. Sometimes we know that these choices far exceed our own and that there is a higher reason for doing so.

I knew that it was a come-to-Jesus moment for me. I needed to come back into His arms. For me, the personal objects were just that—objects. The only hard part for me was leaving our family pictures behind, but even though that may have been hard, I was convinced that it was what we needed to do. Along the way, Cliff continued to question it until the tester came back again, telling us that leaving would be the best decision for us to make.

I could have absolutely, just rested in that moment, but my thoughts kept going back to God and the fact that He was literally moving our family physically and spiritually. I knew then that God was moving us not just to the other side of town, but also moving within us to reconnect with Him in a closer way.

I didn't yet know what that would look like, but when you are a child of God, you know that when He makes big moves in your life, it takes a lot of obedience to understand His purpose for you. It's something you know you don't want to miss because the outcome always puts you in a better place in all areas of your life. It sometimes just takes time to be able to see what He is doing.

As I write the end of this chapter on May 22, 2023, I want to include some notes I took from a sermon Charles Stanley gave a few years back. Here is what he said about obedience to God, "Obedience to God goes far beyond the simple requests He makes to us like a parent, or an employer would. He sees far beyond the limits of our present circumstances. He knows that if we have learned to obey Him in the simple things, then He can trust us with greater challenges. Along with that, He blesses you with new beginnings in your life, and helps you to see later, why He asked you to do the things He asked you to do."[3]

---

[3] Charles Stanley, intouch.org.

7

Starting Anew

Do not conform to the pattern of this world but be transformed by the renewing of your mind. Then you will be able to test and approve what God's will is-his good, pleasing and perfect will. (Romans 12:2)

Ah! This verse! Just after I typed this on March 30, 2021, I remembered a T-shirt I bought from Lifeway when I was a teenager that had this verse on it. I paused in my writing and picked up my phone to see if I could find the same T-shirt online that I had so loved as a new Christian, and yes, I found it! The T-shirt has a group of ugly fish swimming in one direction and the Christian fish swimming against the others with the saying "Go against the flow" and the above scripture written underneath the funny and weird looking school of fish. Lifeway! Ah! What a fun store! It was a place you could find cool Christian merchandise to wear.

After that, I noticed my son, Codie, had come in from work. I took a minute to talk with him in the kitchen. I asked him how his day was as he was making some fresh guacamole. This is something he and I both like. Guacamole is a renewed interest for him, because when he was little, he didn't like it all. It wasn't till a few years ago when he could, as he would say, "really jive with it." As I watched him chop up the onions, I told him about working on this book and shared with him that when we get back from our trip to Myrtle Beach, I will be interviewing some Rosie Riveters along with the World War II vets who I had been previously interviewing for the Library of Congress. I told him about a particular Rosie that I was interested in interviewing. This Rosie started to make planes in 1943 and continued to do so throughout the war. What does this have to do with renewing your mind? Codie asked, "How did these women come back from the war, settle into the home, and just go back to being homemakers?"

Already knowing how this changed women back then, I shared with Him that many didn't. It was a renewing time for them. They were renewed by the new beginnings and opportunities they had experienced, and they grew in their new abilities to work in new capacities. He said, "Yeah! She probably told her husband, 'Hey, I'm not just a cook anymore, I'm an engineer!'" I laughed at his funny sense of humor as we considered the new, exciting feelings these women must have had. Renewed, rejuvenated, reinvigorated—the feelings of new beginnings in their lives that they hadn't experienced before. They knew then that there were new horizons for them, and I'm telling you, you can experience new horizons, too, if you lean into God.

I share these things to show you how you can see God weave events into your day to let you know He is with you. Even now, as I listen to a zoom meeting that a friend sent to me on brain health, I realize that this is another event God has weaved into my day. I'm writing to you about my miracle of being healed from seizures and am listening to a class on essential oils and brain health. This is not a coincidence but God sharing real-life connections.

A couple of years ago when God spoke to me about a hard time I will experience in regard to my seizures, He told me that it will look bad but I will be OK. He also told me that some of my essential oil friends will help me with beneficial essential oils during this time. It's interesting to me that this meeting came on the same day that I am writing this chapter to you. I love how God brings events together in our lives to show us He is here with us. Speaking of the word *essential*, it should be essential for us to pray and ask God to help us to renew our minds daily. That is scriptural guidance, which is God's loving advice to us to help us to remain healthy in our minds and hearts so that we can receive the new beginnings He has waiting for us.

When you think about where we are in our country right now, with COVID-19 and the current division we are facing, don't you think that this would be a perfect time for us as a country to work on renewing our minds and praying for new beginnings for each other? I pray everyday for our country, and for our leaders of our country to be guided by Him and to listen and hear His guidance. I also pray for them to follow in obedience for what God has planned for them to do. The last one is a prayer I pray for me and my family as well.

Speaking of which, interviewing veterans is a project that God told me to do. He said, "Interview as many World War II vets as possible." At the time, I didn't know how I would do it. I didn't have a camera person, I didn't even know how to operate a camera, but I could see the importance of doing it. I understood the need we have to remember people who gave their lives for our freedom, the need for us to remember our country's history, the need to learn about them and their individual stories, and the need to share those stories with others so that we as a nation can become more appreciative of each other. You can see the time in which we are living, and the age of these remaining World War II vets, it's vital that we do these interviews because they will soon be gone. There are other people out there as well, who are taking the time to interview these precious and courageous men and women who served our country eighty years ago.

I do see a connection between the three projects I'm working on: this book, the veteran interviews, and the TV project I'm currently putting together. They all have to do with helping us remember how to connect with each other in better ways, how connecting with

God helps us in our individual life, and how it could help our whole country to connect with each other in a better way. All three of these projects are ones God has asked me to do, which makes me wonder if these projects might lead to more projects that may help our country in other ways later. Hmm.

8

If You Pause to Wonder, You Can See God Working in Your Life

As I write this chapter on April 13, 2021, I wish to explore the topic mentioned in the chapter title and the many pastors, speakers, and church goers who have given testimonies on it. As they look back (that is the pause), they notice where God put specific people or events in their lives to prepare them for the future things that brought together the platform for their testimony.

I shared with a friend of mine, Ron Tripodo, that I was writing this book ahead of the miracle God has promised me. He also heard God tell him in that same loud voice that his wife, Patsy, would be healed. Just as I'm doing with this book, he also "took action" before she was healed. He prayed with the doctors and encouraged them to believe that no matter what the charts said about her grim diagnosis, she would be healed. He also placed some huge billboards up around Atlanta that said, "God is going to heal my wife. Please pray for her." We were reminiscing about that time and how amazing it was to have heard God's voice. We also reflected on how wonderful God's love for all of us is and how He puts people in our lives to help us to see how our lives are interwoven together. It is in God's time, not ours that He moves His hands to make miracles and everyday events happen to help others to know about His wonderful love. Ron encouraged me to press forward to finish my book. He reminded me that the doctors were ready to check him into the funny farm when he shared with them that God was going to heal his wife.

I shared with him that back when we first met them at church and we learned about Patsy's story, I had marveled at not only Patsy's miraculous story but also our friend Yvette Pegues's miraculous story. She is a mutual friend of ours who, after she was healed, became Ms. Wheelchair USA. Both ladies had a medical diagnosis related to the brain, and both ladies were healed. This was amazing to me because your brain is so specially designed by God that when your brain suffers any injury or illness, it can be so hard to heal. That's why both their stories are amazing to me.

Meeting both these women caused me to pause and think about the likelihood of meeting two different people at my church with brain trauma and that God had healed them both. I explained to Ron that my book details how God spoke to me about my own healing, how He would keep my mind intact, and how God said I would eventually have a self-driving car. At that point, I laughed and told him that happened thirteen years ago. He laughed and said, "I don't think they were even developing them back then."

I laughed and replied, "I know, right? Sydney and I saw a TV segment the other day about a company that was getting close to a finished product."

"Kathy, you need to continue to walk in faith, despite what others around you may say. Stay the course and write your story so that you can share it with others and be obedient to the calling God has for you." He added, "You need to claim this, and I will be praying for you that God will completely heal you."

I thanked him and told him that I would. I said, "I think God has more things for both of us to do later to help our country know more about God."

He said, "I hope so. That's what I want to do—help others know about God's love for them."

I replied, "That's all I want to do too." Our conversation ended with us both pausing to wonder what that might be. For now, it is just taking the steps of walking in faith, following God's guidance for us, walking in obedience to what He has for us to do, like writing these books, and waiting to see how He may use these stories to help others know about Him.

I would like to discuss another very important aspect of learning about God as I write the closing remarks of this chapter on June 23, 2021. To learn about God is to not only read His word but to wonder about it. It is to take time to think more deeply about what the scripture means, consider the time in which it was written, and the person who wrote it. Then you should wonder about what God wants you to learn from it, and how to apply what you have learned to your life.

Not too long ago, when I was at a women's event at our church, one of the ladies there shared with me that her and her Bible study group she was in were doing exactly that, they were taking more time to dive into the scriptures and then talking as a group about what they learned, the time it was written, and what the author was writing about. She marveled at how much she was learning from doing that. I shared with her that when I was a teenager and first learning how to study the Bible, I started to do the same thing by using study guides, the Holman Concise Topical Concordance, my study Bible, and other Bible study aids to give me more insight into the scriptures. I have to say that back then, and even now still, it was like finding golden nuggets of treasure to be able to learn more about the different stories in the Bible and the history surrounding those stories. That is how we gain understanding about the goodness of God, how much He loves us, and how he has a plan for all of us. That is how we begin to understand that He has a calling waiting for each of us to step into and live out. I remind my kids off and on about this. We all have a calling in our lives, something that God has uniquely designed us to do, but so many people don't even know that, nor do they stop to wonder. I wonder why that is. That makes me sad to think people might miss their calling and miss knowing God. Again, this is a huge reason why I chose to write this book, so you can see His presence, and His Healing hand working later.

9

God Sends Messengers and Creates Events to Clue You In

It is August 11, 2021, as I write this, and I am recovering from COVID-19. The other day I was resting and was really wishing to not only feel better, but also be able to connect with some of my friends. Then out of the blue, Diana Russell, one of my friends who lives in Chicago, called to tell me that she would be coming to Georgia. This time, for good. I was so excited to hear her voice and her good news. She is always praising God for His goodness, even when going through tough times. I have a few other friends who are like her, and that is what we are supposed to do anyways, right? Anyhoo, while we were talking, I shared with her some of the film projects I have been working on since she had left, and she said, "I will write plays as well."

I marveled at that because I don't see myself as a play writer, but I took it in anyways. She also encouraged me to get ready and prepared (which, as you can tell, I'm doing), to continue writing this book, and to get my TV project ready to launch. Even though I am assured that these projects I'm working on are God-given, it is still nice to hear affirmations and encouragements from friends.

About a week ago, my friend Carolyn and I were talking about how God reveals things to us in different ways. She, too, has heard

God's voice at different times in her life. We were walking to her car from a restaurant where we play cards with some other senior ladies, when I told her about a day when a strange thing happened while Sydney and I had been walking home. We'd found a moth that looked like it was hurt, so we picked it up with a stick. We were going to take it back home to create a safe place for it to feel better. While we were walking home, it started to move its wings and fly. As it flew, Sydney called out to it, "Leafy! Come back!" But just then, a bird swooped down and ate poor Leafy up!

We were stunned and sad, but another strange turn of events happened later that afternoon at home. I looked out on the back porch and noticed that a bird was stuck in the butterfly chair on my deck. We helped free it, then it flew away. I said to Carolyn, "how strange and prophetic that was." When I posted the story on Facebook, another film friend of mine said the same thing.

I shared with Carolyn how I thought the moth represented new beginnings, because our family had been experiencing a lot of those. I still didn't know what the bird part of it meant. After she had gone home, I asked God again what the bird meant to represent. Then I thought about the scripture in the Bible that talks about God replacing what the locusts had eaten and thought that might be part of it. Shortly after, I heard the words "take flight." I realized God was helping me understand that new beginnings in life and with people will happen, and will replace what the locusts had eaten.

To me, that is exciting to think about, and I want you to know that God can do that for you too if you believe He will. I hope that you are encouraged to take flight, not only in your daily life but also in your walk with God. He is an encourager and motivator for me when I sometimes feel frozen and just kind of scared to move. I think we all feel that way sometimes, but when you know God is really moving in your life and has things for you to do, it motivates you to move forward. You also know that He will have great blessings waiting for you when you do what He asks you to do. Yes, you will have hard times, but, just like my friends and I do, you can praise Him in those hard times and feel the comfort of knowing He is there with you.

The take-flight part of it for me is the continuous forward movement of the three projects I've shared with you, because their purpose is to help others and continue to make new connections and friendships. The idea of taking flight is to move forward! Get your feet off the ground, soar to new heights, and fly into new beginnings God has for you.

Sometimes you are also placed in a position to be a messenger too. It works both ways. You can receive insight from God and from others, and sometimes you are the one revealing messages God has laid on your heart to do. I have wanted to know when the right time would be to share with my kids about this miracle of healing that God is going to do for me, and this morning (August 22, 2021) after church, seemed like a perfect time to do so. I wanted to have some kind of good situation for them to receive it in so they would be able to believe in it, and today's message was a good platform for them to maybe believe what I'm saying.

A couple from our church, John and Melissa Fox, have received a miracle from God. John contracted COVID-19 in January 2021 and was in the hospital for 174 days receiving help and care from his doctors. Many people showed up to pray for him and were present during his surgery. They were there to encourage John's family too. Our church, Piedmont, is a fantastic, loving, and supportive church, both to the community and to each individual church member. The kids heard their testimony, and after the sermon was over, I reminded them about our friend's son, Devon, who is now recovering and healing from a twenty-three-foot fall through a roof. He had back surgery, and after just a couple of weeks in the hospital, he is trying to stand up and walk again. I reminded them, too, about how Patsy was healed by God when she had shingles in her brain. I told the kids that God has allowed us to see, and know these people who have received a miracle, and He has put them in our lives to show us that He is still in the business of making miracles happen. I explained that He might be preparing us to see more of His miraculous power unfold.

I reminded them of things I have shared in this book that happened over the last thirteen years, how some of the events have come to pass, and how there are still some things that haven't happened yet, besides my seizures being healed. I reminded them how much He has been there for us, continuously giving us guidance even when we might not have recognized Him doing so. You know how sometimes when you tell your kids something, and they just respond with, "Ok?" That was one of those times, but I am OK with that.

We also talked about the news of the Taliban invading Afghanistan as well, because Pastor Ike touched on that during his sermon, as it is an event that is unfolding right now. It's a historic event not only in the sense of it being world news, but because it is a part of a timeline of events that the Bible talks about happening. When you spend time learning about God and His Word, your perception of the world around you looks different. This is something that when I became a new Christian, I recognized was God's way of showing us His omnipotence and His omnipresence. The scriptures in the Bible align with what we see happening in the world. There are certain sections of the Bible about events that have already happened, some that are happening now, and some that have yet to unfold. That is another way God shows us that the history of the world is "His Story," and He created us to be a part of it while we learn about Him. When we read the Bible, we become aware that we are seeing more of His story unfolding before us.

Is it all good? No, but He loves us so much. He created us to be a part of His Story and gives us opportunities everyday to learn what our part of His Story we are destined to be, and what He has destined for us to do. I hope that by the time you finish reading this book, it piques your interest enough to cause you dig into your Bible and ask Him what His purpose for you is. I also hope you find it and get to live it out!

10

Why Does God Allow Bad Things to Happen in "His Story?"

How many of us have asked this question? As I write this on October 29, 2021, I think there isn't a person out there who hasn't! No one! Jackie struggles with this sometimes because of her spina bifida and being in a wheelchair. Sometimes, but not always, and I know she isn't alone. Every one of us has asked why this or why that when bad things are happening in our lives, or when we see them happen around us. It may be the question of why did my mom or dad leave when I was little? Why did a loved one have to die so young? Why does war have to happen? Why is their division in the hearts of some people? The list of "whys" is endless, and that is not where God wants us to focus our thoughts. We need to break through "those kind of thoughts" so that we don't get stuck on "the why's" in life. I share this with Jackie often—God is not the one making bad things happen, people are, all of us do at some point in time. We are the ones who create sinful actions through our decisions, but God is lovingly there alongside of us as we go through whatever circumstance we encounter. He is there to give us guidance if we ask for His help. Even if we don't, He will still come alongside us and will be there to protect us. He is there to intervene on our behalf when we need His help and rescue us by providing a way out. When we ask for His help, life begins to make more sense. He helps give us clarity about what we should do, and if we listen to Him, it might lead us on to a wonderful new path that is much better than we could ever imagine!

Since the last time I've journaled (which was in August 2021), our Bible study groups have started back up for the fall and I have the pleasure of facilitating one alongside some wonderful ladies twice a year. When it comes to picking out Bible studies to read, learn from, and lead, I always pick the one God lays on my heart to study. It's the same for some of the ladies around me, and I've learned over time, that that's the way it works for some other Christians, too. It is the study you need for the present moment in your life.

The way it works is that you just tend to gravitate toward one specific study as you peruse the different studies that are out there. This time, I chose *Summoned*, a study on the book of Esther. If you know the story of Esther, you might be saying, "Ah, I get it!" For those of you who don't, I encourage you to read it! It is a phenomenal story about the Jews who were almost completely destroyed by Haman the Agagite, who was an enemy of the Jews. He wanted all the Jews to die, but God intervened through a series of events, and people, to help save His children. Esther was placed in a royal position to help save God's people from complete annihilation. It is amazing to me to see how God uses everyday people to bring resolution to sinful, sometimes destructive situations. There is a very memorable part of scripture in Esther that we all can apply to our lives, and that is **Esther 4:14, which says, "For if you remain silent at this time, relief and deliverance for the Jews will arise from another place, but you and your father's family will perish. And who knows but that you have come to your royal position for such a time as this?"**

It is such a beautiful scripture with a meaning that causes one to consider that there is a greater purpose in our lives than just the earthly position we are in now. As I have mentioned before, every time you read the Bible, you get something new out of it, even when you have read the stories again and again. This study is no exception.

Once Haman the Agagite was revealed to be the bad guy, he was hanged on the very pole he had originally put up for Mordecai, Queen Esther's cousin. The bad news for Haman was he didn't know Queen Esther was Jewish, which means he didn't know they were related. The group and I were looking at how the irony unfolds in this story. The bad guy had intentionally created the pole for his nemesis to hang on, but it ended up being his own demise.

Before our group came together for our Bible study this week, I was wondering why Haman hated the Jews so much. I took some time to look up a few commentaries about Haman and why his hate for the Jews ran so, so deep. What I found out, I shared with my group at our next meeting. Coincidentally, the author of *Summoned* discusses this same info later in the study. I never read ahead, so I had no clue she would share the same information later, that I'd discovered on my own. What I found through my research was that back before this time in history, King Saul was told by God, through the prophet Samuel, to attack all the Amalekites and kill them **(1 Samuel 15)**. All of them! Why? Because they were the same group of people who tried to kill the Jews when they were crossing through the parted Red Sea to leave Egypt.

They were always trying to harm His people, so He ordered King Saul to kill them. Why would God want King Saul to do this? Because God knew how much hate the Amalekites had toward the Jews, and He knew what destruction would come to His people if the Amalekites remained alive. The problem was that King Saul was not all the way obedient, and one man, one Amalekite, was left alive. Haman was a descendant of this remaining Amalekite. So you can see how deep the hate ran! They were evil people who just wanted to destroy other people. God knew what would happen to the Jews if just one descendant remained from the Amalekites, a descendant who would become the one Agagite who tried to destroy the entire Jewish nation.

> **As surely as I live, I take no pleasure in the death of the wicked, but rather that they turn from their ways and live. (Ezekiel 33:11)**

Again, this goes back to the idea that He allows each and everyone of us the free will to choose our path, but if we choose to go in the wrong direction, or to be disobedient, He will still find a way to create new beginnings for all of us. As we talked it over in our group, we agreed that this part of trusting God is sometimes hard, but we can remind ourselves that we know that He has good plans for us. **Jeremiah 29:11 states, "For I know the plans I have for you, declares the Lord, plans to prosper you and not to harm you, plans to give you hope and a future."** It is good to remember that when bad people with bad intentions try to destroy others, God will move through those He knows have ready and willing hearts to help others in very important times. One thing's for sure, if His omnipotence did not exist, we, like Queen Esther and the Jews, would all be in big trouble.

11

Knowing God Brings Peace, Joy, and Hope That Can Come from Nowhere Else

As I write this on January 5, 2022, I wish a happy New Year to you all! As we share New Year's wishes with our friends, many of us choose to look to each year with hope and the expectation of new beginnings. Believe it or not, that is the same thing God wants for you every day of your life—new beginnings to help you grow in your walk with Him, new beginnings to help heal and strengthen your relationships with your family and friends that you have now, and new beginnings to look forward to with people you will meet in the future. I don't know about you, but this is something I truly pray for every day, not only for myself and my family, but for others, too. I think this kind of prayer could make a difference in our country. Doesn't it seem like our country and our world desperately need new beginnings to happen?

Do you believe you can experience new beginnings in each area of your life? I do. I know, though, that we need to do our part so that we can experience those new beginnings in life. We can do that when we take the time to renew our minds (Romans 12:2). The beginning of each morning is a perfect time to do so. Don't view each morning as just another day. Each morning can be a special time to have a conversation and devotional with God, which can make a wonderful difference and impact in your day, and for your future, as well.

As I look back at the title of this chapter, it prompts me to think about how cool it is that New Year's is celebrated after Jesus's birthday, a time when we are filled with peace, joy, and love because we are celebrating our Savior's birth. Right after that is a time when we look forward with anticipation to what the new year will bring. Do we ever think about what new things God may have planned to share with us each year? I take a few moments at the beginning of every year, as well as at different times throughout the year, because I am continuously searching for an answer to this question, "What does God have planned for me and my family?" I want to be able to accomplish whatever He has for me to do. I pray every day for Him to reveal to me, my family, and others what His plan is for all of us. I hope He reveals to each of us what His unique plan is, and that we will receive it, and live it out. That would be amazing to see.

April 10, 2022, was Palm Sunday. Our pastor set up communion for us at church, as well as a time for prayer and anointing, followed by a short message about that special day. He had his team of pastors and elders of the church ready at the altar for people to come pray and receive anointing if they wished to ask God for healing. I went forward when the invitation was presented and was surprised when Cliff walked down with me, because when I go to the altar to pray, I usually go alone. We walked over to Nate Galloway, our family connections pastor. He and I had talked when I was at the altar praying the week before. He had been there when I stood up, and I shared with him what God had promised me, and what I needed to pray for. I told him I had four seizures in one day, the previous week, and had fallen down the stairs three times in the last year. I also told him that I was writing this book and how I felt God was initiating events like these to happen before He heals me. I know it seems weird to share that with someone, but I knew Nate would understand because he has also seen miracles happen in his family, too.

One of Nate's younger sons had been diagnosed with retinoblastoma. Miraculously, about two years later, he was declared cancer-free. Besides that amazing news, his second oldest son, Jonah, had previously been diagnosed with juvenile seizures and had recently been declared seizure-free by his doctors. The previous week when we had talked, I told him how happy I was that his son was seizure-free, and how amazing it was that both of his boys received a miracle from God! As we talked about Jonah's miracle, I shared with him that my seizures were inherited from my grandmother, unlike his son's, and how my type of seizures usually skips a generation but can show up again in another family member. We talked about how we know that God can break through even inherited traits to bring healing and life-changing moments into our lives, anytime He wishes to do so.

The one thing I have noticed with our church is that when you have a body of believers actively praying and helping one another in big ways, not just in church, but also in the community, you're going to see God do big things. That is truly what our country needs across the land, don't you think? We need new beginnings for our country to heal and experience a good relationship with God, and our people need new beginnings to experience good relationships with one another too. That's what He wants for all of us.

Pastor Ike often says, "I believe we will continue to see miracles happen in our church, and in our community. I believe we will see entrepreneurs 'rise up' to make a difference in our community and around our country."

I, too, believe that. I hope that my story can make a difference in the lives of those who read it, and that it helps people to grow in their walk with God, or is a starting point for those who have not yet accepted Christ as their personal Savior.

For those of you who have not yet asked Jesus to be your Savior, I hope you do, because the beauty of having God in your life is knowing that new beginnings are there, and will continuously happen throughout your life. My favorite verse is **John 14:6, which says, "I am the way and the truth, and the life. No one comes to the Father except**

through me." The idea that Jesus's words were always so simple and straight forward is, and has always been, endearing to me. No beating around the bush, just showing people this is the way you do it. Just recognize what He did, know He loves you, ask for His forgiveness, and know He died because He loves you so much that He hung on the cross so that one day you can be with Him in heaven. I look forward to that day, but I also look forward to seeing all He still has for me to do here on earth before that time to be with Him in heaven comes around.

12

Opening Yourself Up to See His Timing in Unusual Ways

I received an email from WestBow Press, my publishing company, on May 12, 2022. This company is a well-known, Christian, and family-oriented publishing company. They are a subsidiary of Zondervan and Harper Collins. Both companies have published amazing books over the course of the last century. That is why I had been trying to reach out to them to get this book published.

I'm telling you this because on Friday, May 6, my friend, Carolyn, and I were sitting in my driveway talking after she'd driven me home from our card game. My phone rang, and I recognized the number and asked Carolyn to hang on to her thoughts. As I answered the phone, I noticed that "funny feeling" (which is really, not so funny), coming on. I tried to fight it off, as I always do, but it didn't work. I ended up going into a seizure as I was talking to Gretchen, the publishing consultant from WestBow Press. According to Cliff and Carolyn, I started to talk to Gretchen as I was getting out of the car. I had walked over to the grass from the driveway and had fallen on the ground. Carolyn had gotten Cliff to help, and that night, I found out that Gretchen promised to call me back the following Monday. I was more worried about losing the opportunity to speak with her than I was about the seizure I'd had. I only knew by the tiredness of my body and the lightheadedness that I sometimes get afterward that I'd had one. Now I start to feel the soreness in my body that I get from the falls. Despite how I feel, I worry more about how my seizures affect those around me. I have never liked that. I don't think anyone who has seizures likes how it affects their friends and family when they have them. Isn't that strange, though? They worry about me, and I worry about how it affects them.

Anyway, back to Gretchen. I was thankful when she called back on Monday. She told me about the history of WestBow Press and shared the different publishing options that were available. After that, she asked me what the book would be about. I was honest with her and said, "This may be hard to believe, but the book I am writing is about my miracle that hasn't happened yet." I went on to share with her the timeline of events and how some of them have already happened. I also shared with her Patsy's story.

I was somewhat nervous when I first spoke to her. I was afraid that she might think I'm not all there in the head but was quite surprised as she listened intently. Then she said, "It's funny you are sharing all this with me because I am dealing with shingles right now. They're not in my brain, but I supposedly got them when I fell, and the doctors said that they will probably go away over time."

I replied, "I will pray that they do."

Do you see how God brings others in our lives to form connections? How those connections help you and them to see His hand at work in everything, even if you don't have all the answers yet as to what He is doing? In the meantime, He will give you moments like that to reassure you that you are on the right track, and, depending on how you look at it, you might even see humor in His timing, too. That is what I told Carolyn at church the Sunday after I had my seizure. I apologized for scaring her and added, "God's timing is funny, isn't it? Talking to someone about getting my miracle story published while having a seizure?" We laughed at how uniquely He creates connections in situations to let us know He is there with us. It is up to us to be able to see God's provision and presence and have the assurance that even if we can't see Him with our earthly eyes, we know He is with us. He is creating a timeline of events built on our experiences, both good and bad, to help us move toward the destiny and the purpose that He has waiting for us, and sometimes that means detours might happen before we get there.

13

Connecting Life's Detours to God's Destination for You

MERRIAM-WEBSTER'S COLLEGIATE DICTIONARY DEFINES DETOUR as "a deviation from a direct course or the usual procedure, especially a roundabout way temporarily replacing part of a route." As I write this on May 31, 2022, I wish to expand on this definition in connection with God. The truth is that when you detour off the path of your relationship with God, it sets in motion detours in your life that are ones that can bring stress, frustration, and hurt that might even affect your loved ones. This happens when you make a decision that takes your focus, and your walk, away from God. It could be an enticement of some sort or a worldly desire, like money, greed, recognition, or even a fear of not belonging, not being valued, or not being loved. Sometimes detours are made from pressure from others, which is how the big detour in my life happened. I, of course, made the wrong decision to detour off God's path for me, but my decision was made after almost a decade of being pressured by someone close to me. I will be short about this because I don't want to hurt that loved one. I am sharing this experience so that you might consider how detours away from God can greatly change the course of your life.

Shortly after I accepted Jesus into my heart, I decided that I wanted to become a missionary and travel to different places to help others know about God. This desire began when I taught at Awana, and later when I taught Sunday school. God impressed upon my heart how many people around the world didn't know about Him yet, or maybe did, but didn't have access to the Bible. The problem was that while I wanted to follow God's path for me, I eventually gave in to the external pressure being placed on me.

You may have heard this phrase "when you are going toward the direction God has for you, the devil will try to intervene and stop you or set you on a different course." That is what happened to me. **John 15:13 says, "Greater love has no one than this: to lay down one's life for one's friends."** Laying down your life for another is noble if it's to save a life. But if you're laying down your life for someone's unmet desires, then that is not noble. Yet it happens often. Not just to me, but to some others, as well. It can happen in seemingly small ways, or in big ones. My detour was a big one that caused a lot of hurt for me and my family, but it also taught me much more about giving, compassion, standing beside others, and showing God's love to them. All of which I did before, but it taught me how to stick to it and not give up, when you feel like that is all you want to do. That detour took me out of church for a while, not because I broke any laws or did anything illegal, but due to shame and guilt I had on my part. It was a sin against my own heart, and I knew it was not the direction God had intended for me to go into. Even though I was away from church, I longed for that connection with God. During that time, I knew I was hiding from Him, but I also knew He was there with me and that was comforting to my soul.

Shortly after I had my first child, there was one night that I thought I heard a low, deep voice say, "I am here." I thought, *Did I hear that, or was that just a dream?* I know this all seems illogical, but, in that moment, I couldn't shake the thought I'd truly heard that voice. I knew then, just as I do now, that I'd heard His voice. It's a memory that is embedded in my mind that I think back to sometimes. I know He was reaching out to me then because it was a scary, uncertain time for me and my family. We were experiencing new moments in our lives that were also filled with medical unknowns, doubts, and fears. For me, even though I still felt the guilt of detouring away from God, I felt His peace and reassurance that He was still there, and that everything was going to be all right. It brings an overwhelming peace to me to know that God forgives us of our sins and doesn't hold grudges against us. If only we humans could do the same with each other, in our families, our communities, across our nation, and with others around the world. Maybe if we did so, we might not feel so uneasy about the condition of our country, and the world is in right now.

14

A Few More Thoughts about Our Connection with God

IT IS JUNE 14, 2022, I CONTINUE TO REFLECT ON TIMES OF DETOURS, how God talks to you still, and how He may bring situations to you, sometimes in twos, that cause you to really pause and think, *Hmm….* *that is a stand-out event!* And not only did it happen once but twice! These situations can, no doubt, catch your attention and cause you to wonder, "*This can't be a coincidence; there has to be a reason beyond the circumstance, something for me to learn from these experiences*". It's good to ask God to help you understand what it is He is trying to teach you during moments like these. If you ask Him, He will, in some way, show or tell you what that is.

> **If any of you lacks wisdom, you should ask God, who gives generously to all without finding fault, and it will be given to you. (James 1:5)**

This is one way He teaches us and helps us grow through our earthly experiences, and in our spiritual walk. Without us being able to recognize His presence in our lives, we have no ability to move toward the future He has waiting for us. Even scripture tells us this. **Acts 2:19 says, "I will show wonders in the heavens above and signs on earth below."** So, if He does it, why are we not always recognizing it?

53

Because we get busy. I'm busy, too, but maybe by not having much of a social life, it allowed me to recognize some of these events. It is my hope that as you read about my experiences, they might help you to believe that God is doing the very same thing in your life as well, that He may be helping prepare you for your future with what you've learned from your past. Below, I list the moments events occurred in two's, and what I think God may have been trying to teach me in those time periods.

1. The two moves to different states, first to Texas, and then to Georgia, were during transitional times. Being open to new beginnings helped me see the new beginnings God brought into my life when we moved, geographically, physically, and spiritually. First, learning about Jesus's heritage while I lived in Texas. Then moving to Georgia and learning more about Him, this time, from the Bible. Learning how we, as gentiles, can belong to His family too. I guess, in my case, when I was moved to learn about Him, it caused me to move toward Him, both spiritually and geographically. Incidentally, this is a favorite part of my testimony that I am sharing with you.

2. Learning that both my daughters would both be born with a medical condition. I found out each time when I was three months pregnant, and they were both in the hospital for the first three months of their lives. I can say that during both of those times, I asked God to help them. I also could see that He was giving them each a miracle designed uniquely for their individual needs. I was so very grateful to Him, and I could feel He was there helping them. I trusted that He would. I even told the doctors that they would be OK, even when they told us their diagnoses were serious and their recoveries were unlikely. Did you know the biblical number three means complete and good? You know, anytime a baby is born it is a good occasion. Don't you agree?

3. When the two homes we had were unsafe and how we had to be willing to let go of everything we had. The first time it happened with the house fire, I was shocked, of course, but knew everything could be replaced. The second time, I knew that even though it was a choice to let go of everything, it was more of a choice to put my trust in God's new beginnings, which I did. Learning to let go and trust God is also something we should continuously do throughout our lives.

4. After we moved, we met two Christian friends at church who'd both overcome very severe brain traumas, then shared their testimonies to help inspire others to understand more about God's miraculous power and love. God will also allow me to share my own story of His healing with others before and after He has healed me of my seizures. The hope for the three of us is to be able to help others know about God's unending love for them, how His presence is actively working in our lives, and how He will sometimes show us He is there through the power of His miraculous healing hand. Don't you think that is amazing? I do.

This morning, May 15, 2023, I woke up thinking about how to close this chapter with one last example of how our life experiences are more than just experiences, but are times God is walking with us, and desires for us to want to have a closer relationship with Him. Here is what I did. Since this chapter is about twos, I looked up the biblical meaning for the number two, and it says that it means "to witness." That makes a lot of sense. The Bible is divided into two sections—the Old Testament and the New Testament. When Jesus sent out His disciples, He usually sent them in groups of two so that they could testify together about His teachings and miracles. In the beginning, God created two humans, Adam and Eve, and two of every creature on earth. Then you have God the Father and His Son, Jesus. About the number two, Biblekeeper.com says, "God may be using the number two in your life to gently remind you that He wants you to be a part of a community where you can share the joy of experiencing His spirit."

Family and friends have been a big missing piece in my life for a long time, and I am now truly ready to learn how to be a part of a community. I am ready to see how good it can be when you allow people to be a part of your life. I am ready to embrace what Pastor Ike and Marlon both say often— "We are meant to be in community with each other. We are not meant to be alone." I have always agreed with that and know it is true, and I am finally ready to grow deeper in my friendships with those around me. The number two means to witness, and that is also what I'm doing by writing this book to you.

15

In Our Country, We Protest Too Much, Pray Too Little, and Seek God Even Less

HOW MANY OF YOU ARE FRUSTRATED WITH THE CURRENT STATE of our country? How many of you shake within when you see the pictures on TV or in the media of people walking in the streets protesting for this reason or for that reason? What about the increasing lawlessness across our nation? As I write this on October 11, 2022, these times we are in now are mentioned in the Bible as warnings about what will happen when our nation does not seek God for His guidance. **Matthew 24:12 states, "Because lawlessness is increased, most people's love will grow cold."** We are seeing a lot of this right now in our culture, aren't we? Another verse that connects us with this current time we are living in is **1 John 3:4, which states, "Everyone who practices sin also practices lawlessness; and sin is lawlessness."**

Do we not inquire enough about the current condition of our country? Is constant division meant to be the status quo for our nation? The answer is no! This is not where God wants us to be. If we all ask questions like these, if we really want a better America, and if scripture encourages us to pray for our leaders, why aren't we praying more for them, and for each other?

I urge, then, first of all, that petitions, prayers, intercession, and thanksgiving be made for all people-for kings and all those in authority, that we may live peaceful and quiet lives in all godliness and holiness. This is good and pleases God our Savior, who wants all people to be saved and to come to a knowledge of the truth. (1 Timothy 2:1–4)

When I see what is going on around me, I think of the scene from the movie *Pocahontas* where she is standing in the forest as the two conflicting sides—her people, the Native Americans, and the colonists, come together to fight. In that moment, she yells, "The earth is trembling!" Do you not feel the tremors in our country, and around the world? Why are they here? Because there is conflict everywhere, and without God in our lives, there will be conflict and strife. Why is that? Because we are not as a whole, asking God for His guidance. We are not collectively coming together to pray to Him for ourselves and for each other. We are not as a whole, seeking His guidance, wisdom, and direction in our lives, our neighbors' lives, and our leaders' lives, or for His direction and provision for our country.

I'm not saying that everyone isn't, because there are many, many believers in our country who are seeking His guidance, praying for others, and helping to encourage others to do so as well. But if "We the People" started to include Him through our morning prayer, and if we started devoting some time to being in His Word, then we might begin to see the revival and reunification that is desperately needed in our communities. By being a part of your community and being there for one another, you can make a difference in the lives of others, and maybe even for the sake and the livelihood of our country, too.

What proof do I have that praying, having a devotional time, and seeking God will make a difference in our country? We have *His story* that we call our history to look at. Do you see that God is always there, even inside a word found in our dictionary? Yes, humans came up with that word, but do you see how it can be broken into two distinct parts? I think that is pretty cool! Historically, when leaders of nations did not incorporate God into their lives, or they turned their eyes away from God, their nations always went through hardship. Empires have risen and fallen by the wave of His hand when they chose to turn away from Him. Even His own people are not exempt from this. God has let other nations invade His people's land when they denied Him or turned away from Him. The good news is that He is such a loving God and He is always waiting for us to come back to Him with His arm's wide open. That is why praying is key to making a difference in our country. I will be quick to admit that my prayer life wasn't always that good, but it has gotten a lot better in the past several years, and there is still plenty of room to improve my prayer life. For me now, I don't want to miss my morning prayer time. It is the other part of my quiet time that I enjoy.

Being awakened to God's power is more than a movement; it's a game changer, and it can be positive for the lives of those around you as well. Consider the "woke movement" that is going on around us right now. The woke movement is just that—a movement in a small moment in time. Only a minute piece of history that will be gone tomorrow. Hmm. Being woke to God's power means that we are not easily caught up in a movement based on one's own agenda. Allowing God to move in us is an eternally life-changing movement, and that is something to be woke to, and experience.

16

Consider the Heavenly Realms

> For our struggle is not against flesh and blood, but against the rulers, against the authorities, against the powers of this dark world and against the spiritual forces of evil in the heavenly realms. (Ephesians 6:12)

WHETHER YOU HAVE ASKED JESUS INTO YOUR HEART YET OR NOT, you know there is a heaven where God resides, a fiery place where the devil lives, and between these two places is where we live for now. As I write this chapter on November 16, 2022, I am reminded of when I was a new Christian learning about the fall of Satan from his station as an angel (Isaiah 14:12–15; Ezekiel 28:13–19; Revelation 12:9; Luke 10:18), I thought about how prideful he was for thinking he had more power than God. While reading about the devil being a fallen angel, I also read how some angels wanted to follow him, and they became fallen angels, too. It's weird, but before I even learned of the words "spiritual warfare," when I would hear of bad events happening around us, I would visualize the devil down below stirring things up, laughing at God, and wearing an *I'll-show-you* kind of look. God would respond, "Boy! The wrongs you're trying to do won't ever work! I will always bring good out of the bad situations." God would then give a knowing smile, the look of one who has already seen eternity (because He has) in His omnipotent and omniscient way.

When I was a teenager, I would visualize in my mind how unique His omnipresence is. He can see everyone at every moment and can be everywhere to help anyone, even multiple people in multiple places at one time. Can you visualize that? Think of everyone on the planet. God can see everyone He created at the same time. That is His omniscient, omnipotent love that surrounds us always.

"God looks down from heaven on all mankind to see if there are any who understand, any who seek God" (Psalm 53:2). This scripture gives us assurance that He is with us. Other scripture shares with us ways we can protect ourselves when we are experiencing spiritual warfare. He tells us how we can arm ourselves with the protection that He offers to us freely, and He shares with us how to do it.

> **Finally, be strong in the Lord and in His mighty power. Put on the full Armor of God, so that you can take your stand against the devil's schemes. For our struggle is not against flesh and blood, but against the rulers, against the authorities, against the powers of this dark world and against the spiritual forces of evil in the heavenly realms. Therefore, put on the full armor of God, so that when the day of evil comes, you may be able to stand your ground, and after you have done everything to stand. Stand firm then, with the belt of truth buckled around your waist, with the breastplate of righteousness in place, and with your feet fitted with the readiness that comes from the gospel of peace. In addition to all this, take up the shield of faith, with which you can extinguish all the flaming arrows of the evil one. Take the helmet of salvation and the sword of the Spirit, which is the Word of God. And pray in the Spirit on all occasions with all kinds of prayers and requests. With this in mind, be alert and always keep on praying for all the Lord's people. (Ephesians 6:10–18)**

When you start to do this, you begin to experience how the promises of God allow you to be comforted and help you to move forward in times of darkness and trouble.

Let me share with you today, November 27, 2022, another life moment when the Holy Spirit connected me with God. Today, we watched church at home because it was only one service and there was no Sunday school since it is the weekend after Thanksgiving. After the service finished, I started to fold laundry while listening to a pastor by the name of Dr. Ed Young. He was quoting **Ephesians 6:10–12**. He was talking about how we can win the battle against the devil. He described the appearance of the devil, which is based on what scripture says. He said, "He doesn't have horns but is actually good looking."[4] He is right. The Bible talks about this, and other pastors have described him in the same way. This was something I learned later in life. It takes our entire lives to uncover the truth of God's Word, and it is through His power He shares with us through the Holy Spirit that we discover and receive these life-moment truths.

Let me share a bit more of what Dr. Young said about the spiritual battle that goes on around us. He said, "Paul is telling us there is a real battle going on in the lives of each one of us." **Jeremiah 17:9** says, **"The heart is deceitful above all things and beyond cure. Who can understand it?"** He goes on to talk about how little by little in our lives, the devil will try to invade our thoughts and, through our actions, corrupt our character and turn our thoughts and actions into bad decisions, and bad character. Dr. Young continued, "Rats get through the smallest of places, just the smallest of places. When we look back at these situations where we have gone down the wrong path, we can see the struggle and the devil's strategy, but we can fight it only with the power of God." This takes us back to **Ephesians 6:10, which states, "Finally, be strong in the Lord and in the strength of His might."** That means be strong in His might, God's might! We are only able to fight the devil with the might of God!

To know that there is spiritual warfare around us is to understand that our lives, and the events that happen in it, are yet part of a bigger picture. When we grow deeper in our understanding of our relationship

---

[4] Ed Young, https://winningwalk.org/.

with God, we learn what spiritual warfare is, and what it looks like. When you get into God's Word and learn more about what His Word says, you learn how to identify spiritual warfare. When you pray to God and ask for His guidance, I promise you, He will give it to you. The more you open your heart and make some time in your day to spend with Him, the more you will enjoy getting to know who He is in relation to you. Then the things of this world will be just that—things in this world. The spiritual warfare in our world will not seem so scary because you will have learned to recognize what it looks like, and you will know that God has equipped you to defend yourself against it.

17

The Holy Spirit Lives Within Every Believer

As I write this on December 13, 2022, I am reminded that before Jesus left the earth, He shared with the disciples that even though He was leaving to go to heaven, they would have a piece of Him with them—the Holy Spirit. **"All this I have spoken while still with you. But the advocate, the Holy Spirit, whom the father will send in my name, will teach you all things and will remind you of everything I have said to you" (John 14:25–26).** What He meant was that as the disciples continued to do the work Jesus taught them to do, He would provide them, and fill them with a piece of Himself, which is the Holy Spirit. He told them that the Holy Spirit would be with them to give them the guidance they would need, and the answers to difficult situations that they would encounter later. The presence of the Holy Spirit would be a meaningful part of the conversations that the disciples would have among themselves, and with others as they shared the gospel to all the people they encountered.

This same spirit is within every believer every day, all the time. Do you believe that? If you are a believer, do you ever feel the Holy Spirit living within you? If you are not a Christian yet, isn't it cool to think that God loves each one of us so much that not only did he send His son to die for us to make a way for us to go to heaven, but He also sent the Holy Spirit to dwell in every person as they journey here on earth? He sent the Holy Spirit to be with us as soon as Jesus left the earth to take His seat next to God in heaven. Knowing you get to go to heaven because you asked Jesus into your heart is a comfort all in its own, but knowing that you continuously have the Holy Spirit with you every moment of every day brings a different sense of peace and assurance that you only know when you become a child of God. This leads to the next words that Jesus spoke to the disciples in **John 14:27, which states, "Peace I leave with you, my peace I give you. I do not give to you as the world gives. Do not let your hearts be troubled and do not be afraid."**

What ways can we experience the Holy Spirit, and how can we know its presence? This is a question that takes time to learn the answer to. I will share with you some of my personal experiences that taught me how to identify the Holy Spirit's presence. I can say that I have always been highly sensitive; when I was doing the right things, as well as when I was doing the wrong things, I would feel what I now understand to be the Holy Spirit. However, it wasn't until I asked Jesus into my heart that I could really grow to understand that God placed that sensitivity inside of me. That sensitivity sometimes leads to my conviction, but other times, I have learned, it is guidance that God is giving me. Honestly, when you're being convicted of something, God is trying to give you guidance and a new direction to go in. There are always instances in our lives where we are on the right track, and moments when we are not. Most often, we know which path we are on each day.

The sense of peace felt by the disciples was the assurance of God's presence, even after Jesus left them. He was sharing with them an earthly emotional sense of what the Holy Spirit will feel like in our lives, and that is His peace. His peace you will notice more and more as you learn to trust in Him to guide you. His peace is available every moment of every day, and we can receive His peace when we open ourselves up to believe that the Holy Spirit is real and is advocating for us. I promise you that you will be able to feel the presence of the Holy Spirit when you trust God is with you, both in the good times and the bad times, too.

The Bible verse that tells us this is, **Philippians 4:7**, which says, **"And the peace of God which transcends all understanding, will guard your heart and minds in Christ Jesus."** This verse means that you will feel God's peace in times of not only joy and comfort but also in times of adversity. I can tell you that when you experience extreme times of adversity and a sense of peace at the same time (like I did when we left our house and everything behind), you realize that the sense of peace can override the fearful human nature you may feel during extreme moments in your life. The sense of peace the Holy Spirit gives us is a component of His nature, and His nature is to nurture us and draw us closer to Him.

I've also had experiences where the Holy Spirit reminded me that I was on the wrong path. You know that awkward feeling you get when you're embarrassed? When the blood rushes to your cheeks? To me, that is the feeling I get when I say or do something wrong that I know I shouldn't say or do. That is kind of the same feeling I get when the Holy Spirit is convicting me of something. It can be a small twinge, or it can be such a rush that I feel that awkward feeling coursing through my body in a moment or situation that is not one I should be in.

This sense of embarrassment was first experienced by Adam and Eve after they sinned by eating from the tree of the knowledge of good and evil in the Garden of Eden. After they ate the apple from the tree, they realized they were naked and hid **(Genesis 3)**. The ability to acknowledge sin is in every one of us. So is the ability to acknowledge that the Holy Spirit is within every child of God to guide us in a better direction. God gives us hints of His presence through the Holy Spirit, and sometimes we recognize it right away, while other times it is through hindsight that we see where the Holy Spirit was helping us.

It may seem weird, but other believers have shared their experiences with the Holy Spirit's presence in their lives, too. You know when you hear a person say that they just "had a feeling"? "I felt like I needed to just pick up the phone and call …" or "I had a feeling I needed to go …" or "I had a feeling I needed to check on …" At some point, we have said or heard someone say something like one of the statements above followed by a story of what happened when they did follow up on that hunch, that feeling, which is the Holy Spirit guiding them to "take action" in some way. Usually when you hear the ending to their story, you most often hear a sense of peace that they felt after they "took action." That feeling of peace follows the action taken by the believer who may have unknowingly listened to, and followed the Holy Spirit's guidance. It is so cool when you sit down with others and hear real-life accounts of the Holy Spirit showing up in their lives.

John 14:17 says, "The Spirit of truth. The world cannot accept him because it neither sees him, nor knows him. But you know Him, for He lives with you and will be in you." To me, this scripture is like an invitation. It piques our curiosity and makes us want to know more about the Holy Spirit. Another pastor I like to listen to while I'm walking or playing ball with my dog, Molly, is Dr. David Jeremiah. Dr. Jeremiah said in one of his sermons, "The most basic conviction in life is rooted in the understanding of the nature of God."[5] I believe that, and I believe we can learn so much from our convictions the Holy Spirit gives to us. They are learning tools for life.

The following are some descriptions found in the Bible about the Holy Spirit:

- He is our advocate and teacher **(John 14:25–26)**
- He is a part of the Holy Trinity—the Father, the Son, and the Holy Spirit **(John 16:15)**
- He is known also as the Holy Ghost **(John 15:26)**
- He is referred to as the Spirit of the Lord **(Isaiah 59:19)**
- He is God's Spirit **(1 Corinthians 3:16)**
- He is the Spirit of God **(Genesis 1:2; Judges 3:10; Romans 8:9)**
- He is the Spirit **(John 3:5)**
- He is the Eternal Spirit **(Hebrews 9:14)**
- He is the Spirit of Truth **(John 16:13)**
- He is the Spirit of Grace **(Hebrews 10:29)**

---

[5] David Jeremiah, davidjeremiah.org.

+ He is the Spirit of Glory **(1 Peter 4:14)**
+ He is the Law of the Spirit and gives life **(Romans 8:2)**
+ He is our anointing **(1 John 2:27)**
+ He was involved in the Creation **(Genesis 1:1–2)**
+ He is our Comforter **(Isaiah 11:2; John 14:16; John 15:26; John 16:7)**
+ He is omnipresent **(Psalm 139:7–10)**

The following is what the Holy Spirit does in our lives once we ask Jesus into our hearts:

+ The Holy Spirit gives birth to our spirit **(John 3:5–6)**
+ The Holy Spirit lives in us **(John 14:17; Ephesians 2:22)**
+ The Holy Spirit baptizes us **(Acts 1:5)**
+ The Holy Spirit gives meaning to life **(John 6:63)**
+ He assures us that Christ lives inside of us **(1 John 3:24)**
+ He guarantees we have a future in heaven **(2 Corinthians. 5:5)**
+ He renews us **(Titus 3:4–7)**
+ He seals us **(Ephesians 1:13–14)**
+ He directs us to a life with Christ **(Romans 8:9)**
+ He guides us to truth **(John 16:13)**
+ He helps us pray **(Ephesians 6:18)**
+ He enables us to worship **(Romans 8:26–27)**
+ He helps us to be bold and speak His truth **(Acts 4:31)**
+ He intercedes for us and helps us when we are weak **(Romans 8:26–27)**
+ He provides access to the Father **(Ephesians 2:17–18)**
+ He distributes spiritual gifts **(Galatians 5:22–23; 1 Corinthians 12:1–11)**

There are still more descriptions of the Holy Spirit in the Bible, but I've chosen to end this chapter with the scripture below to share with you that these scriptures, I think, are great reminders that through the Holy Spirit, we can connect with God anytime we need to.

> He came and preached peace to you who were far away and peace to those who were near. For through Him we both have access to the Father by one Spirit. (Ephesians 2:17–18)

18

Prayer Opens the Doors for a Better Connection with God, and with Others

It is January 5, 2023, and I will be honest with you. In the past, my prayer life wasn't the strongest part of my walk with God, and I still don't think it is, but I can say, it is growing stronger thanks to our wonderful Sunday school teacher, Marlon Longacre. He shared a very good model of prayer, which was written by Rick Warren, that I now use every day. It encompasses the different ways that scripture encourages us to pray. It's called "Pray with Your Hands."[6] According to Rick Warren's model, the fingers on your left hand represent who to pray for and the fingers on your right hand represent what to pray for. Let's start with your left hand, and "whom you need to pray for."

- The thumb is located closest to you when your hands are lifted in prayer, and it represents praying for family and friends first.
- The index finger points the way, so praying for our pastors, leaders, and teachers who point our way to God is important. Pray that they will help us to make wise decisions and that God will help them to make wise decisions in their lives too.

---

[6] Rick Warren.

- The tallest finger (your middle finger) is to remind you to pray for people in authority, in our communities, as well as the leaders of our country, and influencers like on social media, and in film. Pray for organizations and businesses, too. We need to pray for them to lead with integrity and to influence others in a good way.

- The ring finger is weak, so it can help you to remember to pray for people who tend to be more vulnerable, like the elderly, sick, and homeless. Pray to God that He will meet their needs and that they might draw closer to Him.

- The pinky finger represents you. Pray for yourself last, after you have prayed for everyone else.

Don't you think this is a pretty cool model of prayer that Rick Warren created? It's easy to remember and use, and it will help you to be able to cover everyone, and every need, in prayer.

Next, is "what you should pray for," and "what it represents," with the fingers on your right hand.

- The thumb is closest to your heart, so pray and ask God to guard your heart because everything flows from your heart. The heart controls your life, so this step is extremely important for you. Ask Him to reveal any sin you need to confess, and for Him to help you to get your heart right.

- The index finger is sometimes representative of the number one, so pray for your priorities and schedule. Ask God to show you what's most important, and for His guidance before you set your schedule.

- The tallest finger is to remind you to pray for your influence over others. Pray that when they see you, they can see how God has worked in your life. Ask God to make you an example of His love and to give you a greater influence so you can use it for good to help others.

- The ring finger helps you to pray for your relationships. Be specific in your prayers to God about the needs of your family, spouse, children, friends, colleagues, supervisors, neighbors, and ministry leaders, and share with Him how you wish to see these relationships grow, or heal, and how they can bring glory to God.
- The pinky finger is to remind us to pray for material blessings. Rick Warren writes, "There is nothing wrong with asking God for material blessings. It's not the most important thing, so it's the last thing you pray for." **James 4:2 reminds us, "You do not have, because you do not ask God."** I have learned that when our hearts are sincere in the things we ask for and we follow God's guidance for us, God will answer our prayers according to His will for our lives, and scripture also says that will happen.

Today is January 8, 2023. It was our first Sunday school class of the year. This morning, Marlon spoke about the goodness of God. I mention this because during our study time together, **James 4:2** was mentioned. Likewise, Pastor Ike referred to **James 4:2** on New Year's Day when he spoke with us about the prayer of Jabez. I am sharing this with you as another example, just like the others in this book, of how cool it is to see God connect His goodness with us in so many ways.

A bookend scripture for James 4:2 is **Psalm 37:4, which states, "Delight yourself in the Lord and He shall give you the desires of your heart."** So, when you share your needs with God, and you do what He asks you to do, you become amazed at what you see He is doing in your life. I am ever so grateful for the things we have, but as a child of God, I know that nothing outlasts the love you can have by knowing God and having Him in your life. That is priceless and eternal.

Rick Warren's model "Pray with Your Hands" has helped me immensely by showing me a new way to write out my prayers, adding my specific needs, as well as the needs of those around me, then praying for them each morning during my quiet time. Thank you, Rick Warren, for this great model of prayer, and thank you Marlon, for sharing Rick Warren's prayer with us in class.

Even though I shared this model with you earlier this week (today is January 10, 2023), we know this is only one method of prayer. Everyone has their own unique way of praying, and that is a beautiful thing because it lets God see and hear from all His children in different ways. Can you imagine Him looking down at all of us, watching us pray to Him?

Consider this, if we as a people, one nation as a whole, a nation that was founded on praying to God, where leaders pleaded for the foundation of our country to be blessed by God, begin to pray individually, and together for each other, and for our leaders, we just might become more indivisible as a nation, and possibly more connected with each other, and most importantly, being more connected in our relationship with Him. What a positive difference that would make, right? It's the difference we need, and deep down we all want to see more positivity and unity in our country, and with one another. Truly, prayer changes everything, and we can all make a difference when we "Pray with our Hands" and our hearts, taking our requests to God.

It is February 17, 2023, and this last part of prayer I'm adding to this chapter is something I am just now discovering. When you pray for people who you know need help, but you have not met, there may come a time later when you get to meet them and see where God is working in their life, and maybe, just maybe, a new friendship can be born through God, and through your prayers for them. Wouldn't that be great?

I have one more question for you. Did you know prayer is also a form of worship? We have the book of Psalm that tells us the answer is yes! While we worship God, just like David did, He can bring healing not just to our physical bodies, but also to our mental, and spiritual health too. David enjoyed praising and singing hymns to God, and I love singing hymns and worshiping Him, too.

19

Experience the Healing Hand of God

As much as I thought this chapter would be about the belief and assurance of my promised healing from God, I'm writing this on February 16, 2023, at a time when both of my girls are struggling and need healing in their lives too. They need individual healing in different ways. Ways such as physical healing and emotional healing, but it is spiritual healing that allows all aspects of oneself to heal. This is true for all of us. As I have mentioned before, during times of pain and unknowns, we can be filled with fear and uncertainty. Those unknowns are insecurities that can take hold of us if we let them, causing us to feel like we can't move. It is during those times that we need to refocus our attention on God. When we do that, we can see God move in the midst of adversity. How does this work? When we put our trust in Him, it lifts our burden of fear and allows us to see beyond the current situation. My mom and I both talked about how we see Him moving in my daughters' struggles to hopefully help bring them healing, and maybe our whole family healing, too. That's a continual prayer that I've had not just for them and our family, but for other families who need His healing hand in their lives as well.

A real-life example of someone in the Bible who focused their attention on God and worshiped Him during hard times was Leah.

Leah was the sister of Rachel and the unloved wife of Jacob, yet she knew God was showing love to her each time she gave birth to a son. Children were something that her sister, Rachel, was not blessed with until later. Though she didn't receive love from Jacob, she knew God loved her and wouldn't forget about her. The reason you could tell that she knew God loved her was the fact that she praised God and worshiped Him every time He gave her another son. She worshiped God, praised Him, and thanked Him throughout her life.

Because Leah focused on God's blessings, she was able to see the legacy He was creating through her for generations to come. **2 Corinthians 4:18 states, "So we fix our eyes not on what is seen, but on what is unseen, since what is seen is temporary, but what is unseen is eternal."** She also enjoyed the blessings that she received through her sons, which filled her heart with love. I think God's love also gave her feelings of contentment knowing that her children would have a very important and eternal legacy in His family. What she did not know was that later, beyond her lifetime, she would become the matriarch of two very important tribes of Israel. Judah, which is the tribe Jesus came from, and the tribe of Levi, which is where some of the spiritual leaders, like Moses and Aaron, came from. Part of God's power to heal is one of the heart. I think He did that for Leah, and I know He is still in the business of healing hearts today.

As we talk about the different ways He heals, sometimes He sends angels to intervene when we need help. I will share with you a true story that has just happened to show you this is real. My friend Carolyn, who I've mentioned before, just a few months ago, physically experienced a hand pushing her out of harm's way. This is not some colorful story I'm adding to this chapter; this really happened. She explained that she was getting out of her car when it started to roll back over her. There was no one around, yet she felt a hand pushing her out of the way. She was still hurt a little, but it could have been so much worse if God hadn't intervened. She knew it was God moving in that situation, either Him or one of His angels pushing her to safety. Miracles are still happening every day. Isn't God awesome?

When God heals, sometimes it takes time, and sometimes He does it instantly. For me, God has told me it will take a little time. It will also take some work, which it did for some of the people who I have mentioned in this book who've received miracles from God—Patsy, Yvette, John, Devon, Carolyn, and Pastor Nate's two sons. The reason we go through hard things in life is so that we can become better, stronger, and, hopefully, closer to God. It is also to share with others His amazing power to do the impossible. Faith in seeing is easy to believe, but walking in faith when you can't see God means you are putting your trust in Him to be there for you while believing He is there, which, as you can tell as you read this, I do. Likewise, I hope you do, too.

20

Planning, Preparing, and Believing Are Actions of Faith

BEFORE I SHARE WITH YOU HOW I AM PREPARING MYSELF FOR THE miracle God has promised me, let's first look at some people in the Bible who believed God, and took actions of faith before they witnessed the miracle event God had promised would happen in their lives. Today, March 14, 2023, I will share with you what they did ahead of their promised miracle and how they responded to what God asked them to do. The way we respond to God when He asks us to do something is very important. The response God looks for is an action. Just like our parents or our boss at work expect us to move when we are asked to, so does God. I am going to share with you four people in the Bible who "took action" ahead of a miracle. Of course, there are so many more people who have responded to God's instructions, and subsequently witnessed promised miracles, but I am going to focus only on these four people who were in the family of God.

The first person of faith I will talk about is Moses. God told Moses to take the Israelites and leave Egypt. This was a big step of faith, having to gather a whole nation of Israelites and leave Egypt with a huge army of soldiers following behind them. This had to be scary, but with God's help, they were able to subdue the pharaoh's army until they reached the shores of the Red Sea **(Exodus 14)**. As Pharaoh's army quickly grew closer to them, Moses called out to the Israelites, **"Do not be afraid! Stand firm, and you will see the deliverance the Lord will bring you today. The Egyptians you see today you will never see again"** (Exodus 14:13). Moses boldly spoke up in faith, both to the Israelites and to the Egyptian army. He spoke it into existence so that he and the Israelites would have the courage to walk through the parted waters of the Red Sea.

I just realized that this example of faith in Moses's story fulfills the scripture **Isaiah 43:2, which states, "When you pass through the waters, I will be with you."** I personally love this scripture so much that we have an oil painting with it on our wall in our home. Moses's action of faith is as noted above. He called it out, he declared it would happen because he heard God's voice, and actively moved as God directed him to.

The second person who showed faith is Joshua during the battle of Jericho **(Joshua 6)**. Here you have a small army marching upon a fortified city. This seemed like an impossible win in the eyes of both Joshua's army (at least to some of the soldiers), and the people of Jericho, who laughed at them. The Israelites were given instructions to march around the city for six days. Then on the seventh day, they obediently followed God's simple instruction to blow their horns. They saw the walls of the city fall before their eyes, just as God had said would happen. Because they did what He said, they were able to declare a victory over the Promised Land, which they dedicated to Him. Joshua and his fellow soldiers' actions of faith were that they trusted, believed, and followed God's instructions exactly as He had told them to do.

The third person of faith is David, a preteen who had the courage and belief in God to fight Goliath. He was a little shepherd boy going against a big giant who mocked and laughed at him and the Israelites. David became the target of one of Goliath's mocking sessions when he brought food to his brothers **(1 Samuel 17)**. Once he saw how Goliath made fun of the Israelite soldiers, and he noticed that they were too afraid to make a move, he went to King Saul and proclaimed to Saul that since God had previously delivered him from lions and bears, he knew He would protect him in battle against the towering Goliath. David's faith was unshakeable. His action of faith was that he recognized God's presence in the past, as well as the present. He reminded others of His omnipotence and gave credit to God for what he had done in his life, and what He was about to do for the Israelites. He proclaimed God's deliverance with tiny stones in his hands and, at the same time, proclaimed to everyone how mighty the rock of salvation is.

> **The Lord is my rock, my fortress and my deliverer; my God is my rock, in whom I take refuge, my shield and the horn of my salvation, my stronghold. (Psalm 18:2)**

April 10, 2023, the day after Easter. Lastly, we have another preteen who was appointed to a long-awaited royal position that many hopeful young Israelite ladies wished to receive. This blessed preteen was Mary, Jesus's mom. We know she grew up in a family of believers. That is only part of her story. She also had great faith in God and had the willingness, desire, and heart to serve Him. This had to be a core part of Mary's life and character before she became Jesus's mom. I think having the influence of her older cousin Elizabeth, and Elizabeth's husband, Zechariah in her life, helped her to grow in her love for God and encouraged her to wonder, and look forward to the promised Messiah who would uniquely become both her child and her Lord. Can you imagine what she must have thought about that? She took note of God's miracle that He had blessed her elderly cousin with. The miracle was a son, who was known as John the Baptist, and who was Jesus's cousin, too. **(Luke 1:5–56).**

I think that miracle was an affirmation for Mary that in less than a year, she would also receive a blessing, and meet God's promise to all of Israel, and to the world. When the angel Gabriel told her that she would be the mother of Jesus, her response says it all about her servant's heart. "**'I am the Lord's servant,' Mary answered. 'May your word to me be fulfilled'" (Luke 1:38).** Her action of faith was that she simply believed. She was willing to serve Him without any hesitations or reservations.

That is what God is looking for in all of us. I think we need to be able to look for it within ourselves too. I think if we all did that, we would probably be extremely amazed at the work God could do through us, and the blessings we would receive by taking actions of faith while trusting and following Him.

The thing is, God knows our heart and sees the person we are from the time we are born because He created us. He sees our heart and searches for those who are willing to serve Him. Have you ever taken some time to imagine God looking for people across the earth who are willing to serve Him? This is something I thought about when I was younger, and sometimes even now. I think it is special and amazing that God sees the heart of each, and every one of us. Just as Moses, Joshua, David, and Mary were willing to serve God during their lives, we should be willing to do the same now by taking action with our faith. What a difference it would make in our lives, as well as in the lives of those around us. **Jeremiah 17:10 says, "I the Lord search the heart and examine the mind, to reward each person according to their conduct, according to what their deeds deserve."**

One other thing about Mary, and the others who I've mentioned, is that they all wondered about the things God told them to do, then had the blessing of witnessing, and being a part of the miracles God performed in their lives. The big thing is, they trusted Him and believed in His promises to them before He revealed the promises and miracles for them and others to see.

One of my actions of faith that I've taken before my miracle happens, besides writing this book, has been to write down a list of things for my family to help me to do each day to help me to get back to my old self when that time comes. It is just a list of normal everyday things I do now, that my family will need to help me do later. This list is on my table next to my bed. It is something God told me to put together, and it makes sense to me! My friend Ron had to do that for his wife, Patsy, when she was relearning how to do normal everyday things again during her recovery from having shingles on her brain.

Another thing I have done is place books on my shelf near my bed. Some of them are about how to improve your memory, another one is about other people's miracle stories, and a book of prayers for healing. I have put them there so that maybe they might be helpful to me when that time comes. There are still other things I need to do, like journal the events that happen each day. This one is hard for me right now, because I'm busy working on this book, as well as the other two projects I told you about. Journaling is a good thing to do because it helps you to remember little moments that overtime, you might otherwise forget. Plus, those memories will be written down so that you will be able to share them with your family, as well.

My last action of faith is hope. By writing this book ahead of my miracle, I hope it will bring others closer to God. Our country, and our world, really need to draw closer to Him to be able to experience the miraculous healing power and love He has waiting for each, and every one of us. I hope this book helps you to "take action" and make God a daily part of your life. I also hope that I've been able to show you some good examples of God's goodness, and love that He has shown me, and others, and how He has the same love for you, too. He loves you, and is there for you every day, whether you know it or not. I hope you know it. If you don't yet know, I hope you decide to begin to search for Him by reading the Bible and praying, while you learn for yourself how amazing and wonderful He is, our omniscient, loving, Heavenly Father.

Leaving You with Final Thoughts from This Side of My Miracle

I write this final chapter on April 24, 2023, and I hope you were able to glean from this book some of the wonderful ways we can experience God's presence in our lives and recognize the ability we have, to reach out to and learn more about Him every day. When we create a quiet time, we open a door for a relationship with Him. That quiet time helps us to grow in our love for God. The other part of our relationship with God is being able to experience the presence of the Holy Spirit that is always with us once we have asked Jesus into our hearts. When we continue to stay connected to Him, we become more aware of how He gives us guidance and affirmations in our daily lives, whenever we may need it. The power that prayer has may not be noticed right away, but over time, it makes an impact in our relationship with God, as well as in our relationships with others. Prayer time is our talk time with God and is also time we get to spend worshiping Him.

We also begin to realize that if we take moments to pause in our daily lives, it helps us to take in the events that we see unfolding before us, both good and bad. That is a God-given gift given to us through the Holy Spirit. The Holy Spirit helps us to become aware of God's presence through the things we see, through affirmations, through His peace that He gives when chaos surrounds us, and even through times where we have taken wrong turns, and He convicts our hearts to get us back on the right track.

We learn that the word *conviction* means discipline from God, and it can be a time for us to reflect and grow in our lives by learning from our mistakes. We also become aware that conviction can be a positive affirmation that God gives us to move us forward in a positive direction in our lives.

As we grow closer to God, we begin to understand that those moments of conviction can steer us toward a brighter future, and the purpose God has waiting for us. We also learn that when we step into that brighter future, we can look back to see the discipline He gave us was with love, and was given to help us to learn, and then share with others what we have learned from our walk with Him.

By seeing examples of people in the Bible who faithfully followed God's instructions, we see how they got to experience the power of God in ways that may seem unimaginable to us. When they walked in faith and "took action," even when they didn't understand how they would accomplish the tasks God had given them, it led to them trusting God more and increased their faith in Him. Another blessing they received by walking in obedience and faith with God was the blessing of being able to live out, see, and experience what their purpose here on earth was.

Pastor Ike says in some of his sermons that "sometimes your greatest doors of opportunity swing on tiny hinges called obedience." To me, that is a very profound and true statement. A statement to truly consider, and actively receive as a child of God. Obedience to God is what can move you forward toward your legacy and calling in life, the purpose He designed for the unique you that you are.

I don't know about you, but I want to know my purpose God has for me and be able to live it out to the fullest that I can, according to His will. I pray this every day for myself, for my family and friends, and for everyone else too. I pray that those of you who read this learn what your purpose God has specifically for you is, and that you will be able to walk into it and live it out completely. The choice, of course, is yours if you choose to seek it out or not. We are all free to choose to follow Him or not. I hope you consider how very important it is to trust God, and how much our world needs people to believe in God. It is very important for your future to trust in Him now, so that you can live for eternity with Him in heaven one day, and I pray that you do.

May God bless all of you who read this book, and may you trust Him enough to move in faith toward Him, and the purpose He has ready for you, whatever that is.

Thank You, God, for loving us so much that You gave Your Son for the forgiveness of our sins so that when we decide to believe and trust You, we can experience eternal life with You. Thank You, God, in advance for the miracle You will give me, and thank You for allowing me to share this miracle with others in advance. May this miracle bring healing to not only myself, but also to others around the world who not only have the need for physical healing, but for emotional, and spiritual healing as well. In Jesus' name I pray, Amen.

I will end this book with a word my friend Trudy Simmons shared with us at a women's event a couple weeks back. She ended the night by saying, "I pray everyone has a supernatural moment with God." I love that, don't you? She is such a sweet and wonderful woman of God. Her prayer is what I pray for you too. May you also see how precious His love is for you, and may you be able to experience "supernatural moments" with Him in your life as well.

Blessings to you all,
With His love,
Kathy Puder